How to Draw DINOSAURS

**Illustrated by
Georgene Griffin**

kidsbooks®
Incorporated

Copyright © 1997 Kidsbooks Inc.
3535 West Peterson Avenue
Chicago, IL 60659

Manufactured in the United States of America

Visit us at www.kidsbooks.com
Volume discounts available for group purchases.

S0-BFB-073

INTRODUCTION

This book will teach you how to draw many different types of dinosaurs. Some are more difficult to draw than others, but if you follow along, step by step, then (most importantly!) practice on your own, you'll soon be able to draw all the dinosaurs in this book. You will also learn the methods for drawing anything you want by breaking it down into basic shapes.

The most basic and commonly used shape is the oval. There are many variations of ovals—some are small and round, others are long and flat, and many are in between.

Most of the figures in this book begin with some kind of oval. Then, other ovals, shapes, and lines are added to form the basic dinosaur outline.

Most times a free-form oval is used, like the ones pictured below. In addition to ovals, variations of other basic shapes, such as circles, squares, rectangles, triangles, and simple lines are used to connect the shapes. Using these basic shapes will help you start your drawing.

Some basic oval shapes:

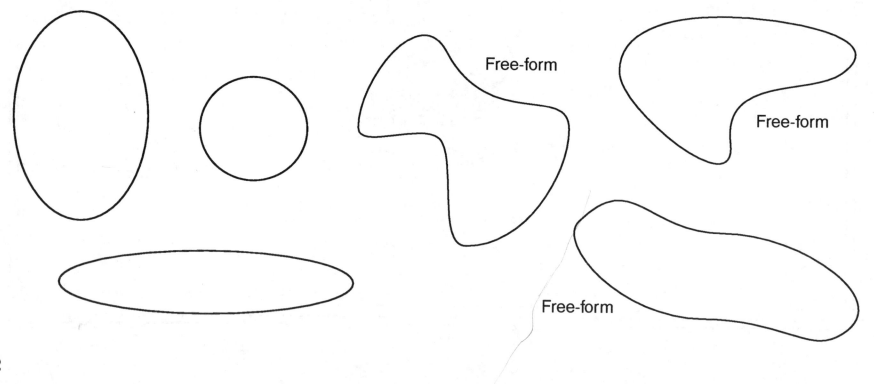

Free-form

Free-form

Free-form

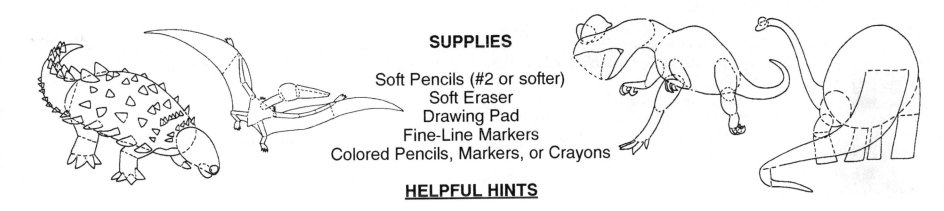

SUPPLIES

Soft Pencils (#2 or softer)
Soft Eraser
Drawing Pad
Fine-Line Markers
Colored Pencils, Markers, or Crayons

<u>HELPFUL HINTS</u>

1. Following steps 1 and 2 carefully will make the final steps easier. The first two steps create a solid foundation of the figure—much like a builder who must first construct a foundation before building the rest of the house. Next comes the fun part—creating the smooth, clean outline drawing of the animal, and adding all the finishing touches, details, shading, and color.

2. **Always keep your pencil lines light and soft.** These "guidelines" will be easier to erase when you no longer need them.

3. Don't be afraid to erase. It usually takes a lot of drawing and erasing before you will be satisfied with the way your drawing looks.

4. Add details, shading, and all the finishing touches after you have blended and refined all the shapes and your figure is complete.

5. Remember: **Practice Makes Perfect**. Don't be discouraged if you can't get the hang of it right away. Just keep drawing and erasing until you do.

HOW TO START

Look at the finished drawing below. Study it. Then study the steps it took to get to the final drawing. Notice where the shapes overlap and where they intersect. Is the eye over the corner of the mouth or behind it? Look for relationships among the shapes.

1. Draw the main shape first—usually the largest. In this case it is a large, free-form oval for the body. Then draw an oval for the head and connect it to the body, forming the neck. Using basic shapes add arms and claws.

2. Carve out the dinosaur's mouth. Sketch additional basic shapes for the legs and tail.

3. Blend and refine the shapes into a smooth outline of the dinosaur's body. Add the sharp teeth. Keep erasing and drawing until you feel it's just right. (The dotted lines indicate that they will be erased in step 3.)

Tip: Dotted lines indicate that they will be erased in following steps.

4. Add lots of lines for shading and skin texture.

Or you may color your drawing with colored pencils, markers, or crayons.

Sometimes it's helpful to start by first tracing the final drawing. Once you understand the relationships of the shapes and parts within the final drawing, it will be easier to do it yourself from scratch.

Remember: It's *not* important to get it perfect. It *is* important for you to be happy with your work!

Erasing Tips
• Once you have completed the line drawing (usually after step #2), erase your guidelines. Then proceed to add details, shading and/or coloring your drawing.
• Using a permanent, fine-line marker over your pencil guidelines will make it easier to erase the pencil lines.
• A very soft or kneaded eraser will erase the pencil lines without smudging the drawing or ripping the paper.

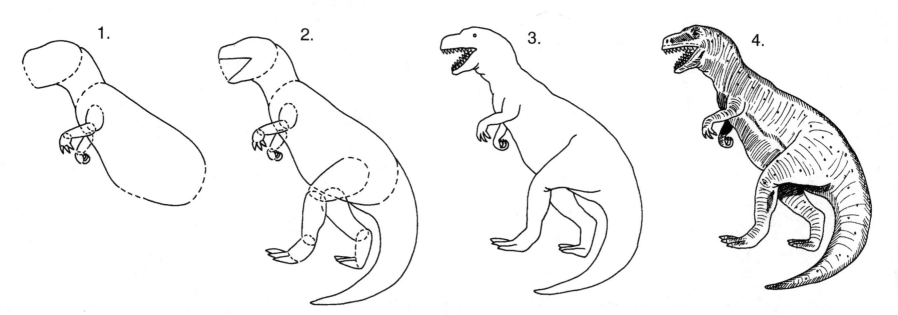

BASIC DINOSAUR CLASSIFICATION

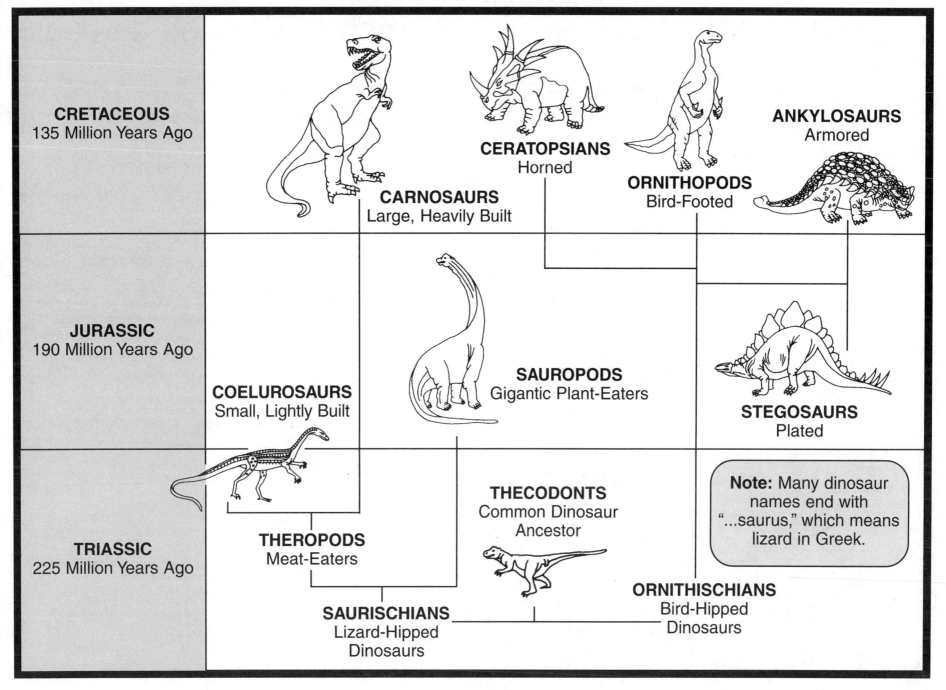

CRETACEOUS
135 Million Years Ago

CERATOPSIANS
Horned

ANKYLOSAURS
Armored

ORNITHOPODS
Bird-Footed

CARNOSAURS
Large, Heavily Built

JURASSIC
190 Million Years Ago

COELUROSAURS
Small, Lightly Built

SAUROPODS
Gigantic Plant-Eaters

STEGOSAURS
Plated

TRIASSIC
225 Million Years Ago

THECODONTS
Common Dinosaur
Ancestor

Note: Many dinosaur names end with "...saurus," which means lizard in Greek.

THEROPODS
Meat-Eaters

SAURISCHIANS
Lizard-Hipped
Dinosaurs

ORNITHISCHIANS
Bird-Hipped
Dinosaurs

Mamenchisaurus

(mah-MEN-chee-sawr-us)

Named for the area in China, Mamenchi, where its fossils were found. Until the 1980s, Mamenchisaurus was thought to have the longest neck of any animal. It was 36 feet long.

1. Begin by lightly sketching the basic oval guideline shapes for the body and legs.

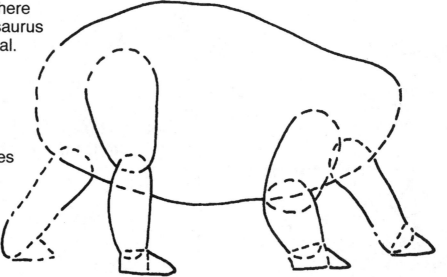

2. Draw a simple shape for the head. Connect the head to the body with two long lines, forming the neck. Add the long, curved tail.

Note: Always draw your guidelines lightly in steps 1 and 2. It will be easier to erase them later.

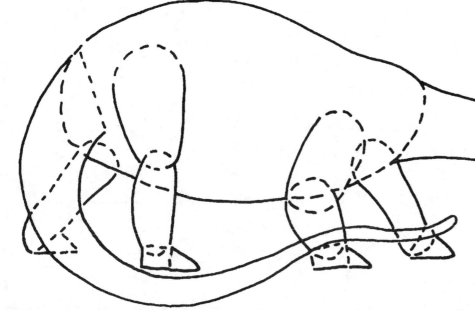

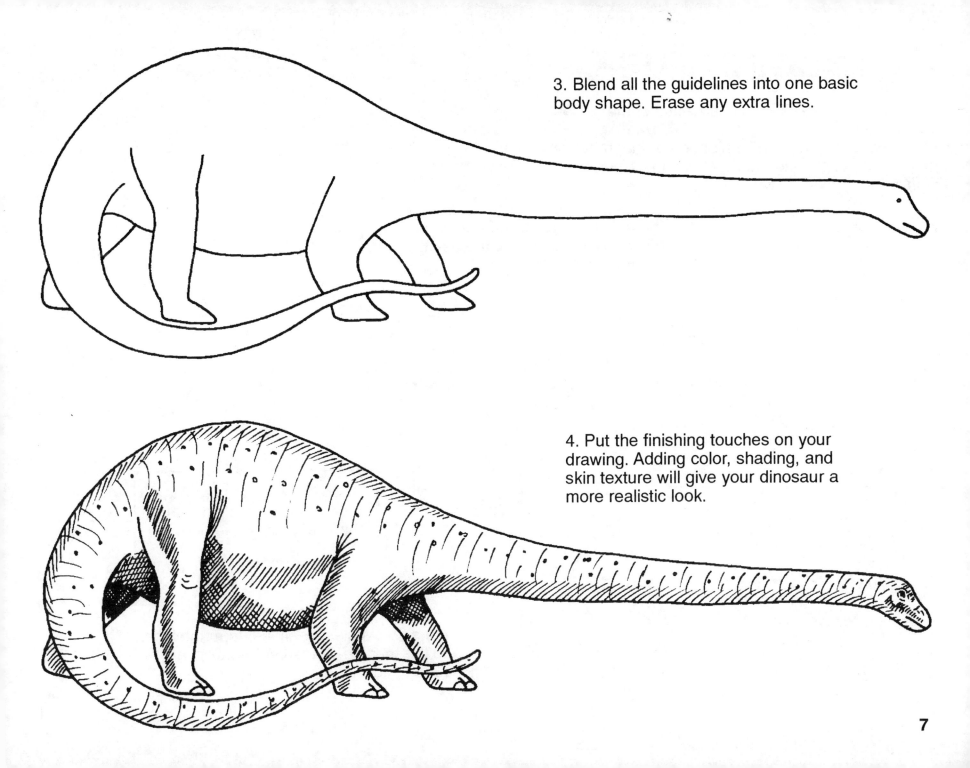

3. Blend all the guidelines into one basic body shape. Erase any extra lines.

4. Put the finishing touches on your drawing. Adding color, shading, and skin texture will give your dinosaur a more realistic look.

Styracosaurus

(sty-RAK-uh-sawr-us)

Means "Spiked Lizard" because of the spikes on its head.

Styracosaurus was a plant eater that may have lived in herds, grazing the fields like the American buffalo of the modern world.

1. Start with a large free-form oval for the body. Add shapes for the head, lower jaw, and pointed "beak."

Keep drawing and erasing until you are satisfied with the way your picture looks.

2. Next, using simple guidelines, form the legs, tail, and the triangle-shaped spikes on the dinosaur's head.

3. Add an eye with a small spike above it as shown. Combine the shapes into a smooth outline of the body. Now you're ready for the finishing touches.

4. Complete the eye, and beak. Then, add lots of shading and skin details. You can even add some ground for the Styracosaurus to stomp on! For a dramatic effect, try going over the outline with a felt-tip pen.

Mosasaurus

(MO-zuh-sawr-us)

Means "Meuse Lizard," after the Meuse River in The Netherlands where it was found.

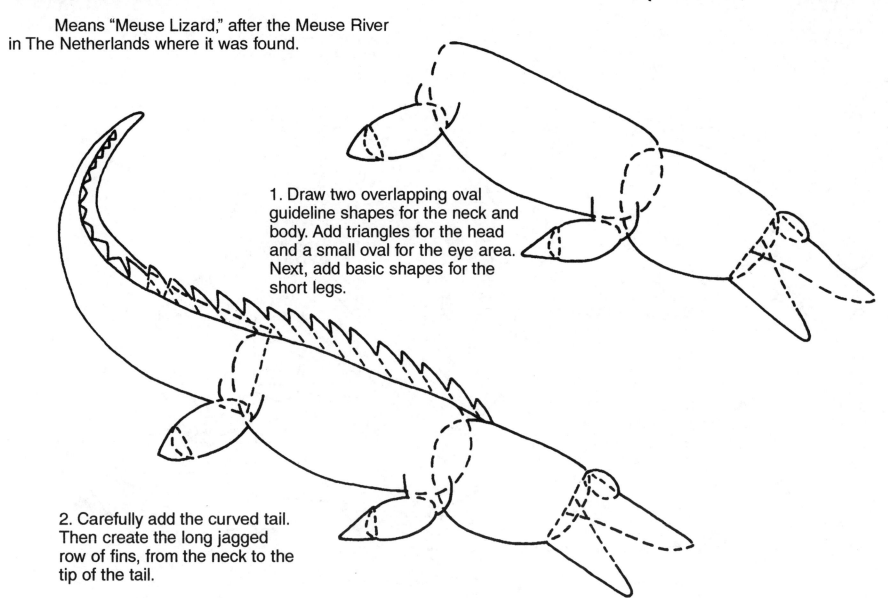

1. Draw two overlapping oval guideline shapes for the neck and body. Add triangles for the head and a small oval for the eye area. Next, add basic shapes for the short legs.

2. Carefully add the curved tail. Then create the long jagged row of fins, from the neck to the tip of the tail.

10

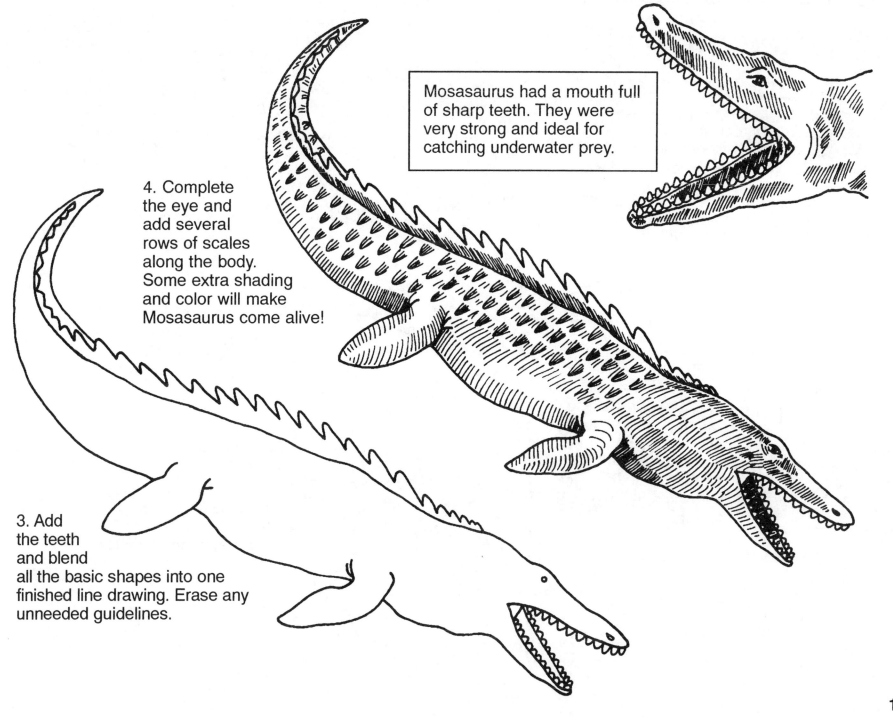

Mosasaurus had a mouth full of sharp teeth. They were very strong and ideal for catching underwater prey.

4. Complete the eye and add several rows of scales along the body. Some extra shading and color will make Mosasaurus come alive!

3. Add the teeth and blend all the basic shapes into one finished line drawing. Erase any unneeded guidelines.

Ornithomimus
(or-nith-uh-MY-mus)

Means "Bird Imitator" because it resembled an ostrich. Ornithomimus was very speedy and quickly ran away from danger.

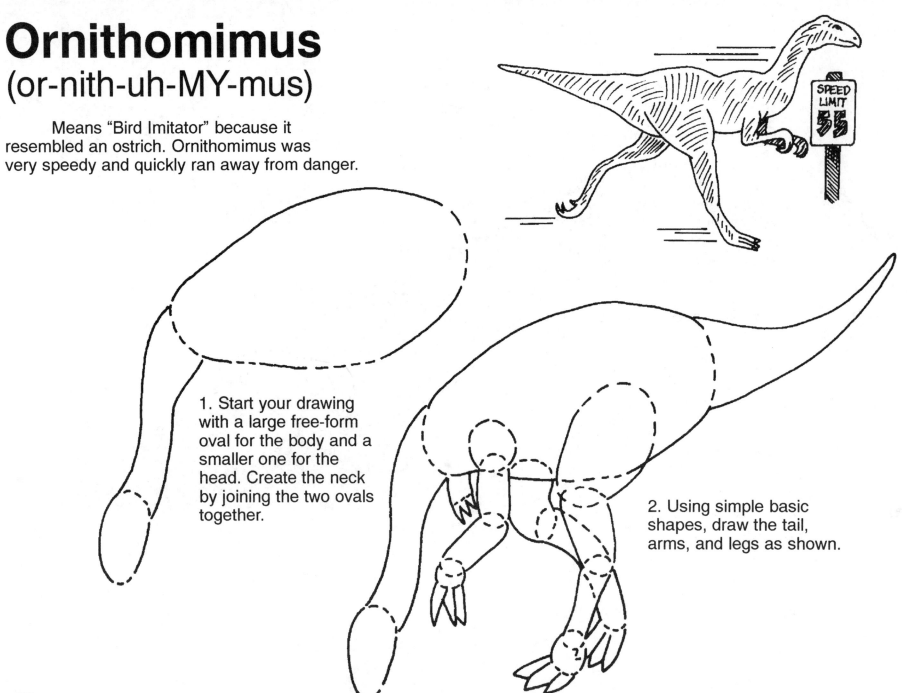

1. Start your drawing with a large free-form oval for the body and a smaller one for the head. Create the neck by joining the two ovals together.

2. Using simple basic shapes, draw the tail, arms, and legs as shown.

SPEED LIMIT 55

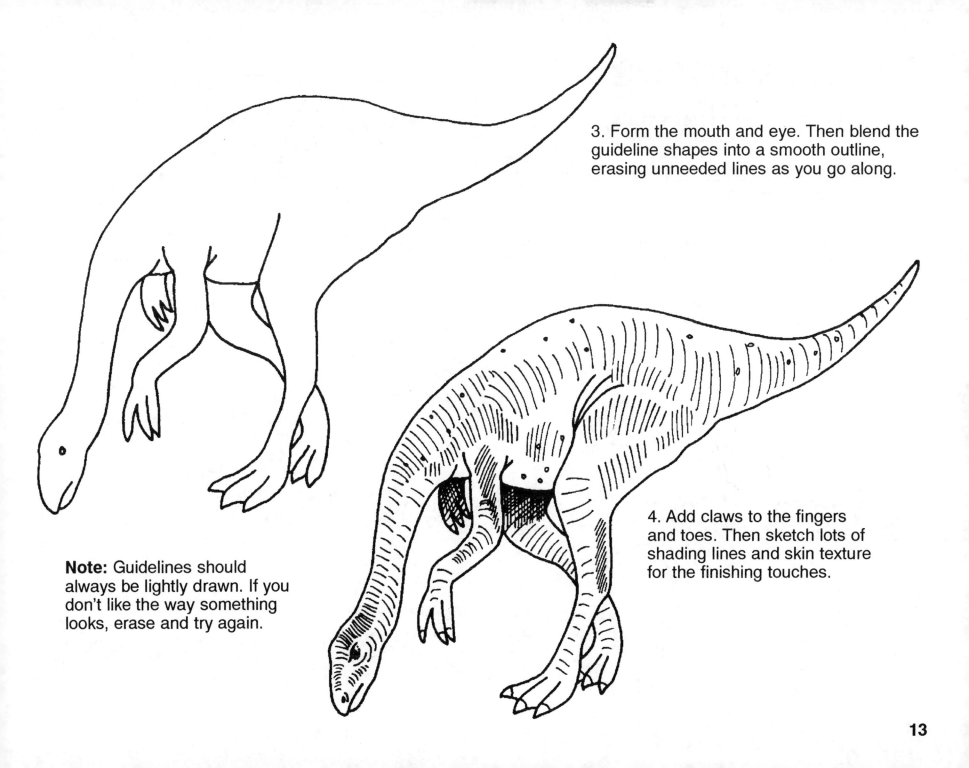

3. Form the mouth and eye. Then blend the guideline shapes into a smooth outline, erasing unneeded lines as you go along.

Note: Guidelines should always be lightly drawn. If you don't like the way something looks, erase and try again.

4. Add claws to the fingers and toes. Then sketch lots of shading lines and skin texture for the finishing touches.

Palaeoscincus
(pay-lee-o-SKINK-us)

   Means "Ancient Skink" because its tooth resembles that of a modern skink. Palaeoscincus was discovered when scientists found one tooth in Montana.

Note: Steps 1 and 2 are very important. They establish the overall structure and look of your drawing. In steps 3 and 4 you are simply refining and adding details to the figure you have created in steps 1 and 2.

1. Begin this unique dinosaur with a large oval shape for the body and two overlapping circles for the head. Attach the tail, adding two egg-shaped ovals at the tip.

2. Add the legs and claws. Next, carefully add rows of triangle-shaped spikes all over the body and tail. Don't forget the four spikes protecting the head.

14

3. Complete the face and blend all the separate shapes into a smooth outline of the dinosaur's body. Be sure to erase any lines you no longer need.

4. Now use your imagination to fill in the details. What color or colors do you think this dinosaur was? No one really knows, so use your favorite colors to complete Palaeoscincus.

15

Diplodocus

(dih-PLOD-uh-kus)

Means "Double Beam" because of the Y-shaped vertebrae on its tail. A complete skeleton of Diplodocus measured 90 feet from head to tail. Many of this plant-eater's bones have been found in the Rocky Mountain states of North America.

1. By drawing Diplodocus at the angle shown, you can get a better sense of how gigantic this dinosaur was. Start with a very large oval for the body. Add a small circle for the chest and a small oval with a circle on top for the head. Connect the head to the body with two long lines, forming the neck.

2. Draw the rectangular-shaped legs and attach the huge, curved tail.

3. Add the eye and mouth. Then blend all your shapes into one finished outline drawing. Erase any extra lines.

4. Add details, scenery, and color. You may want to create a scene by drawing several different dinosaurs in a prehistoric setting. (See pages 120-121)

Note: Before going to step 4, make sure you are satisfied with the way your drawing looks.

Alectrosaurus

(ah-LEK-truh-sawr-us)

Means "Lizard All Alone" because it was the only Asian meat-eater of its kind when first found.

Alectrosaurus is the slimmer meat-eating cousin of fierce Tyrannosaurus.

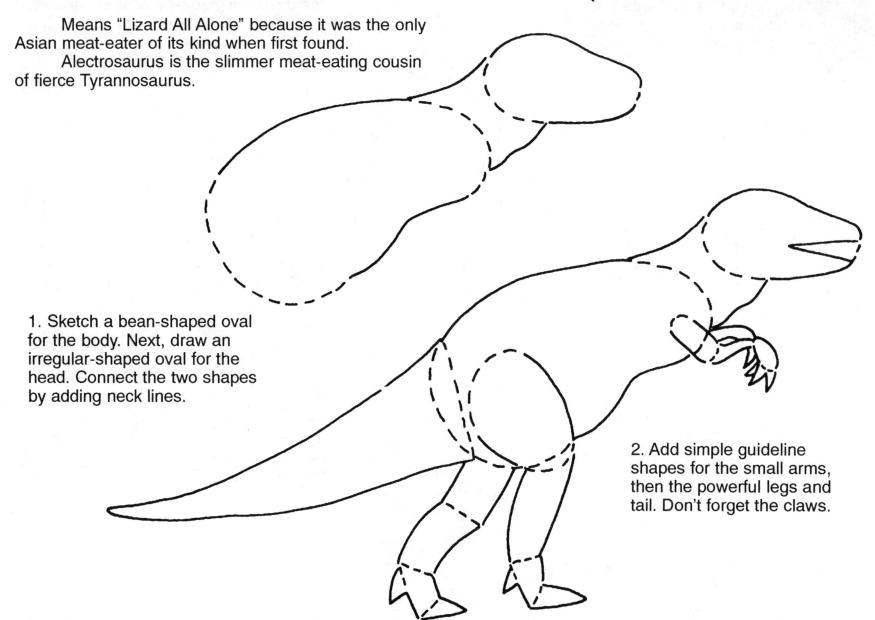

1. Sketch a bean-shaped oval for the body. Next, draw an irregular-shaped oval for the head. Connect the two shapes by adding neck lines.

2. Add simple guideline shapes for the small arms, then the powerful legs and tail. Don't forget the claws.

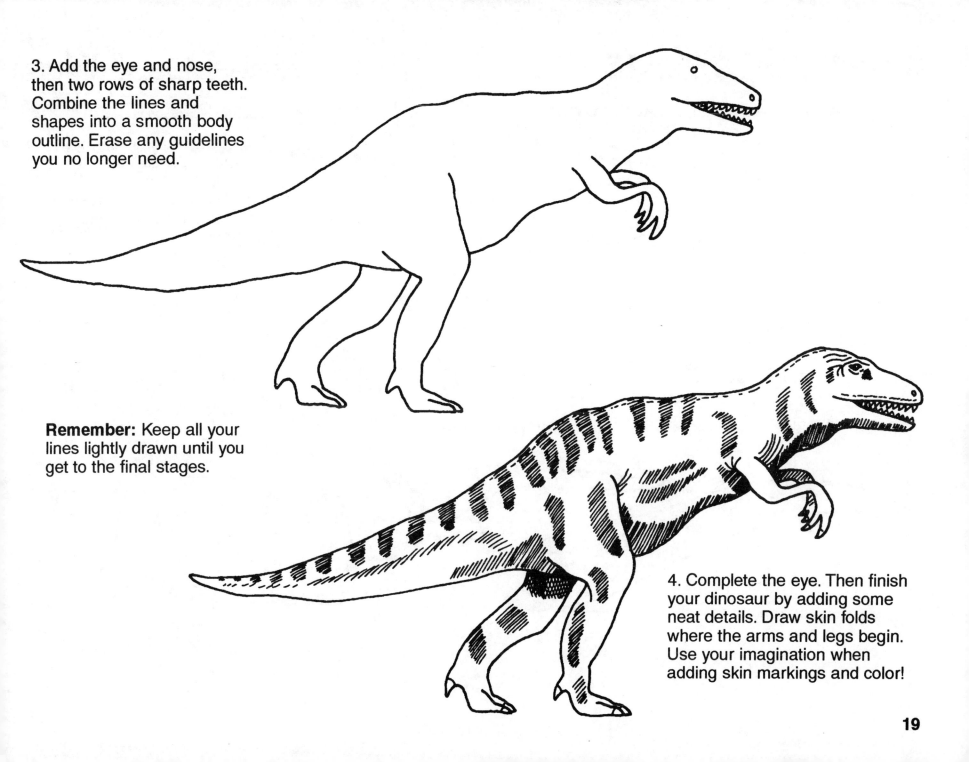

3. Add the eye and nose, then two rows of sharp teeth. Combine the lines and shapes into a smooth body outline. Erase any guidelines you no longer need.

Remember: Keep all your lines lightly drawn until you get to the final stages.

4. Complete the eye. Then finish your dinosaur by adding some neat details. Draw skin folds where the arms and legs begin. Use your imagination when adding skin markings and color!

Quetzalcoatlus

(ket-sol-ko-AT-lus)

Named after Quetzalcoatl, the Aztec feathered serpent god.

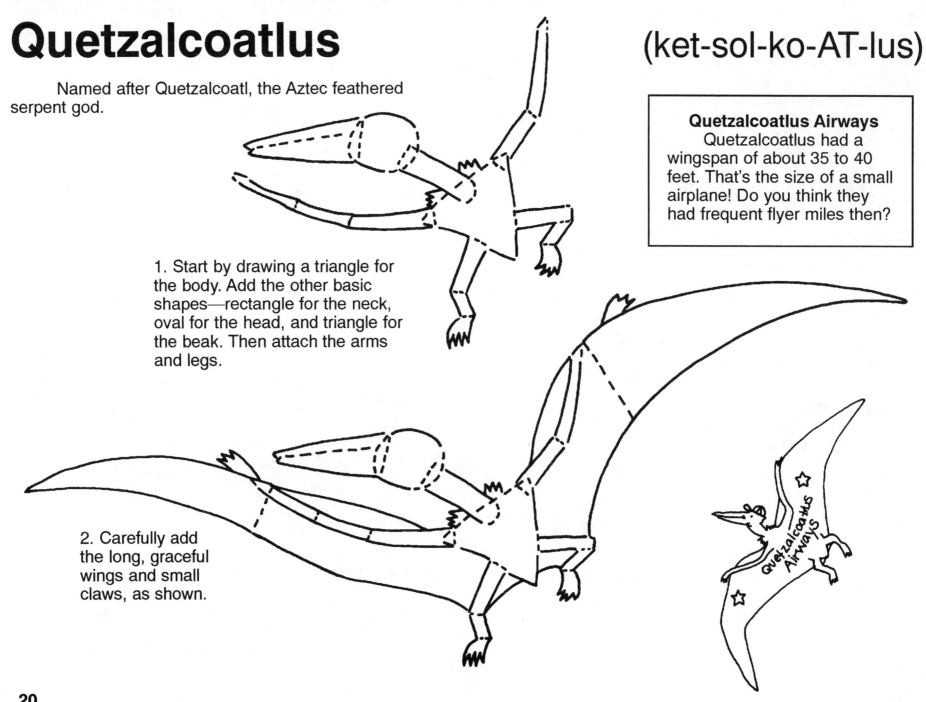

Quetzalcoatlus Airways
Quetzalcoatlus had a wingspan of about 35 to 40 feet. That's the size of a small airplane! Do you think they had frequent flyer miles then?

1. Start by drawing a triangle for the body. Add the other basic shapes—rectangle for the neck, oval for the head, and triangle for the beak. Then attach the arms and legs.

2. Carefully add the long, graceful wings and small claws, as shown.

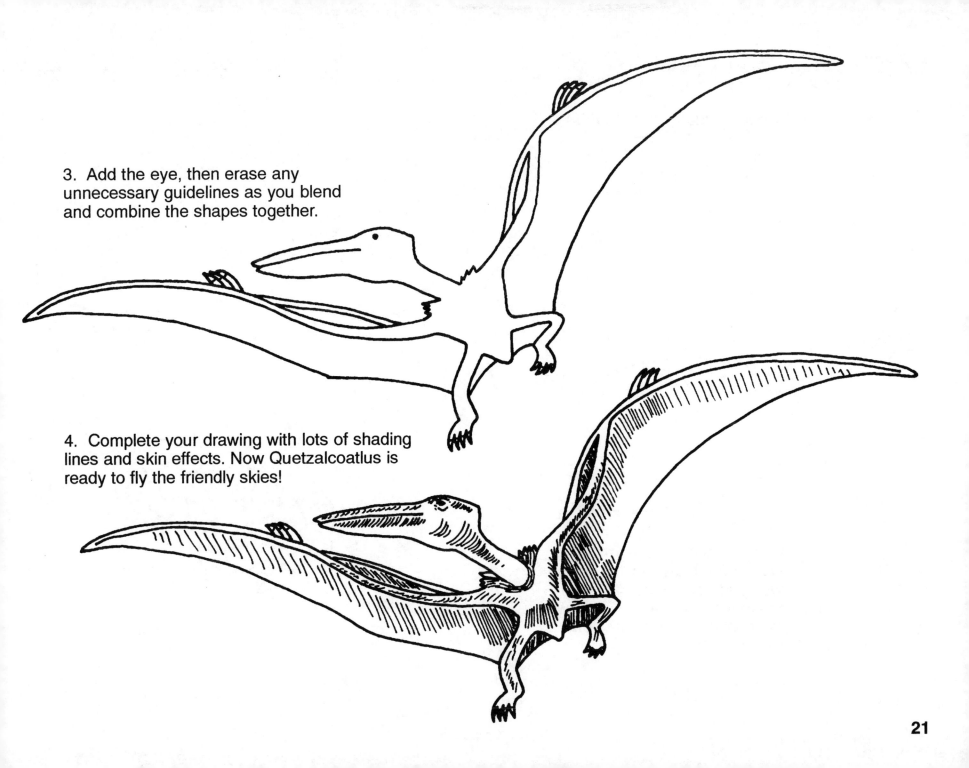

3. Add the eye, then erase any unnecessary guidelines as you blend and combine the shapes together.

4. Complete your drawing with lots of shading lines and skin effects. Now Quetzalcoatlus is ready to fly the friendly skies!

21

Velociraptor

Means "Swift Robber" due to its quickness and grasping hands.

If Velociraptor was cold-blooded, its skin would have been similar to a lizard's. If it was warm-blooded, it may have been covered with feathers or fur.

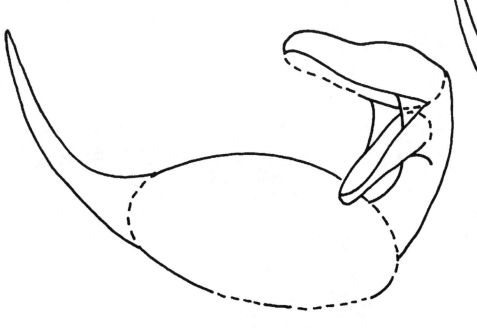

2. Using simple shapes draw the arms, legs, and claws. Note the upturned claw on the feet.

1. Lightly sketch an egg-shaped oval for the body. Next, using oval guidelines, very carefully create the upper and lower jaws and connect them to the body. Then add the tail.

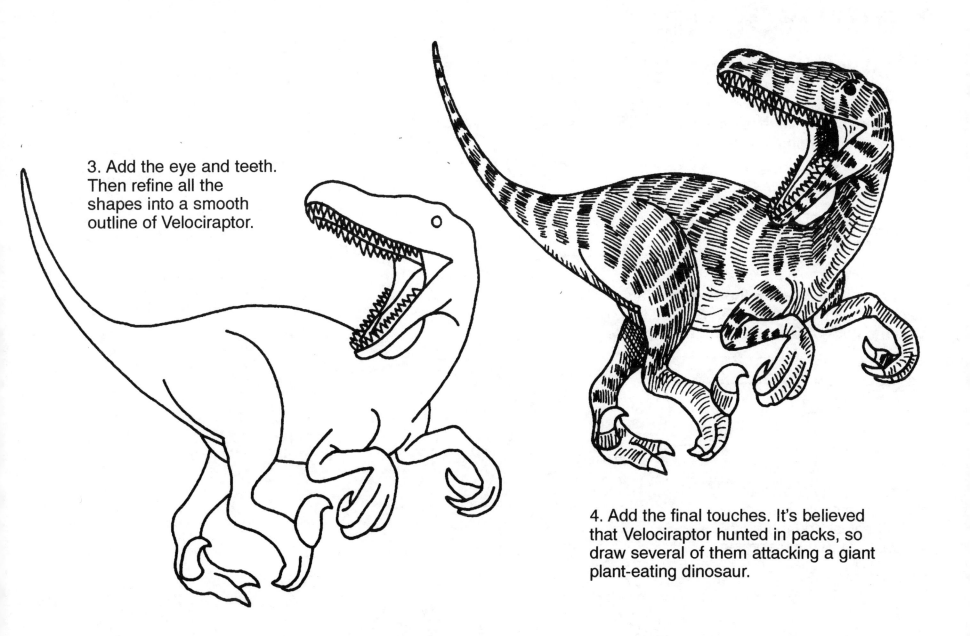

3. Add the eye and teeth. Then refine all the shapes into a smooth outline of Velociraptor.

4. Add the final touches. It's believed that Velociraptor hunted in packs, so draw several of them attacking a giant plant-eating dinosaur.

Hadrosaurus
(HAD-ruh-sawr-us)

Means "Bulky Lizard" because of its big size.

In 1868, a plaster skeleton of Hadrosaurus was the first ever put on display.

Note: It's usually easier to begin any drawing by sketching the largest shape first.

1. Draw a large oval for the body and a smaller, pointy oval for the head. Connect the two ovals to form the neck. Attach a long triangle for the tail.

2. Add a line for the mouth. Next, using ovals, rectangles, and triangles, add the guideline shapes for the arms and legs.

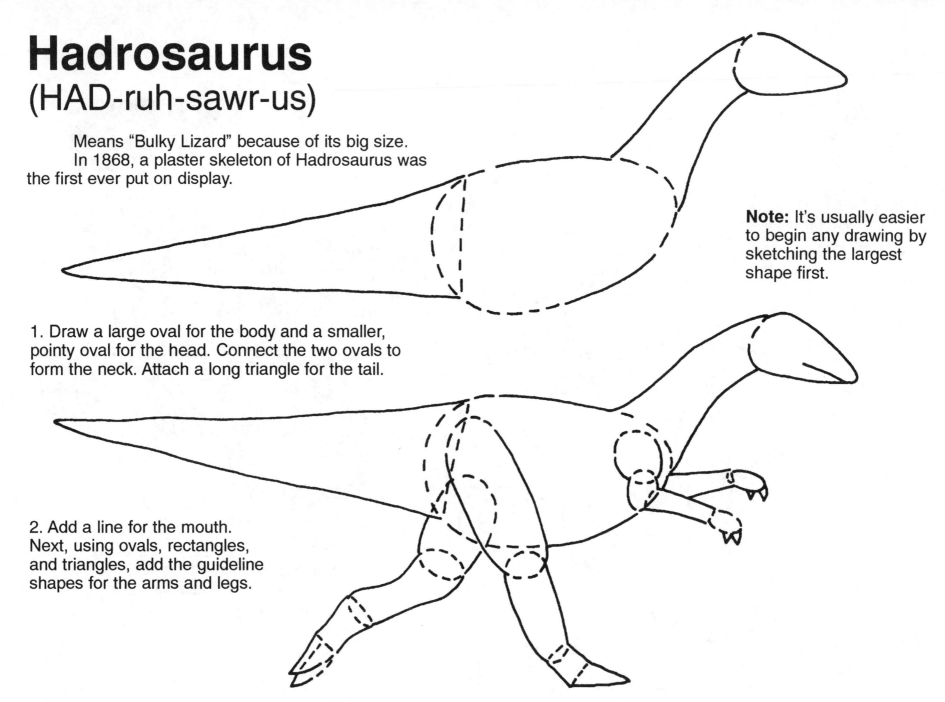

3. Add the eye, then blend the shapes into a smooth body outline. Note the flattened snout. Keep erasing and drawing until you're satisfied with the way your dinosaur looks.

4. Create the pointy claws and complete the eye. Then add lots of shading, skin wrinkles, some color, and scenery to complete your picture.

Ceratosaurus
(sair-AT-o-sawr-us)

Means "Horned Lizard" because of the horn behind its nose. Meat-eating Ceratosaurus was found at the scene of a crime in Wyoming! Its broken teeth were lying next to a fossil of a Camarasaurus skeleton.

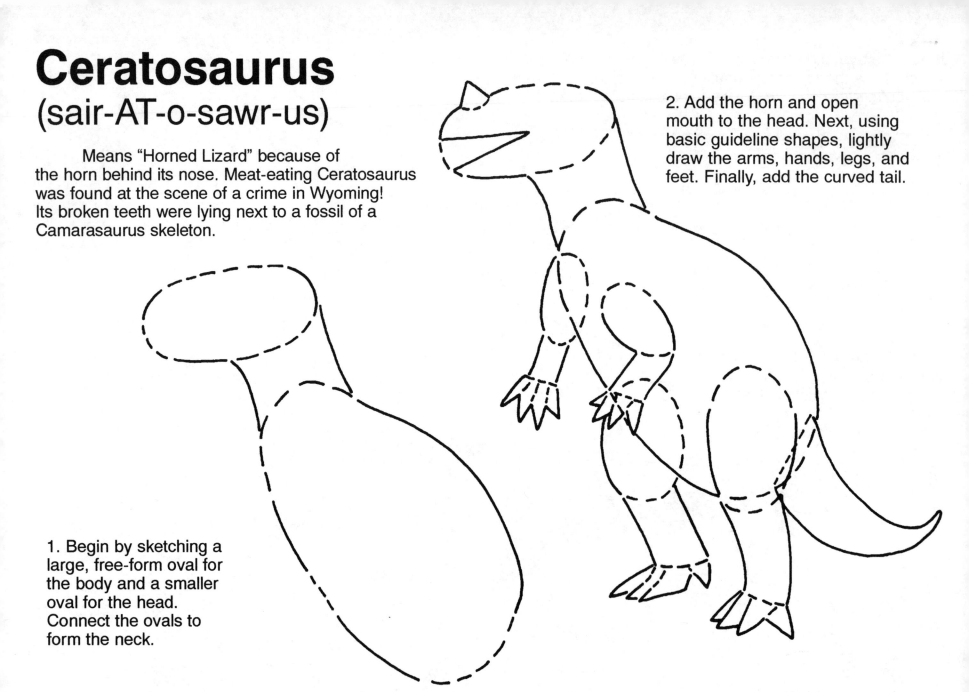

2. Add the horn and open mouth to the head. Next, using basic guideline shapes, lightly draw the arms, hands, legs, and feet. Finally, add the curved tail.

1. Begin by sketching a large, free-form oval for the body and a smaller oval for the head. Connect the ovals to form the neck.

3. Add the eye and sharp teeth. Then blend all the shapes together, erasing any unneeded guidelines.

4. Add details and shading for the finishing touches. You can outline Ceratosaurus with a black felt-tip pen or color it with your favorite colors.

Iguanodon
(ig-WAN-oh-don)

Means "Iguana Tooth" because its teeth resemble those of an iguana lizard.

About 140 million years ago, a large number of Iguanodon drowned in a lake that ran across northwest Europe. Many fossils have been found in this "Iguanodon graveyard."

2. Add the basic shapes for the arms, legs, pointy claws, and tail. Note the spike pointing upward on top of each hand. Don't forget the mouth!

1. Start with a large free-form oval for the body. Add a smaller oval for the head and a triangle shape for the neck. Connect the neck to the body with a short line, as shown.

3. Add an eye and a nostril. Erase any unneeded guidelines as you blend the shapes and lines into a smooth outline of Iguanodon.

4. Complete your drawing by adding rows of shading and skin details. Now this Iguanodon is ready to pound the prehistoric pavement!

Note: Make sure you have built a solid foundation with the first two steps before going on to step 3.

Avimimus

(a-vee-MY-mus)

Means "Bird Mimic" due to its birdlike appearance. Some scientists believe Avimimus was similar to the modern-day roadrunner, and that it might have even had feathers!

1. Lightly sketch a free-form shape for the body. Add the head, neck, and tail as shown.

2. Draw some simple shapes to create the arms, claws, legs, and feet. Shape the head and define the open mouth.

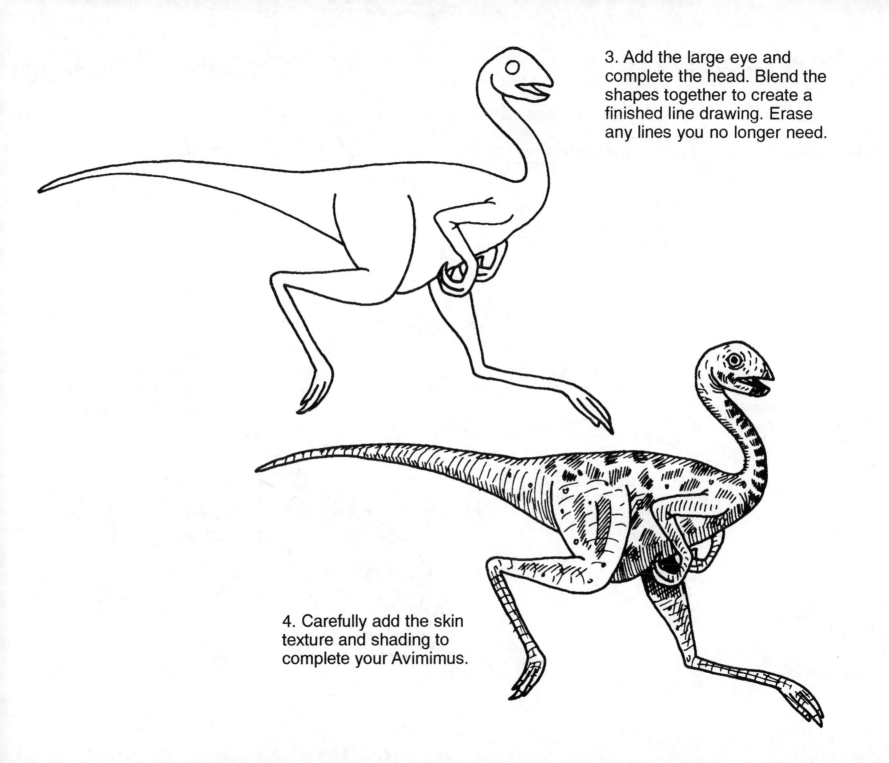

3. Add the large eye and complete the head. Blend the shapes together to create a finished line drawing. Erase any lines you no longer need.

4. Carefully add the skin texture and shading to complete your Avimimus.

31

Ichthyosaurus

(ik-thee-uh-SAWR-us)

Means "Fish Lizard" because of its fishlike appearance. Ichthyosaurus was a prehistoric sea reptile, not a dinosaur. Unlike dinosaurs, Ichthyosaurus gave birth to live young.

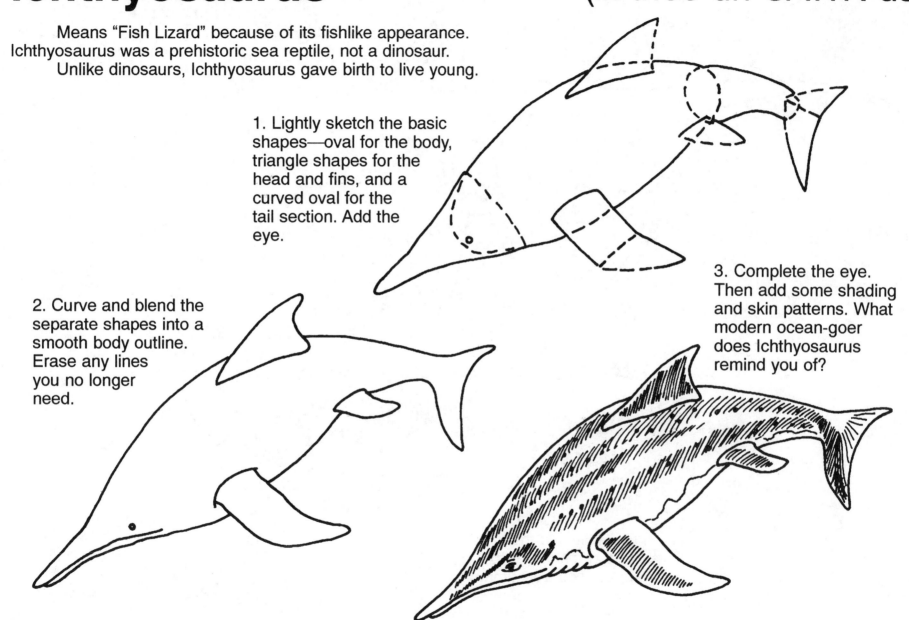

1. Lightly sketch the basic shapes—oval for the body, triangle shapes for the head and fins, and a curved oval for the tail section. Add the eye.

2. Curve and blend the separate shapes into a smooth body outline. Erase any lines you no longer need.

3. Complete the eye. Then add some shading and skin patterns. What modern ocean-goer does Ichthyosaurus remind you of?

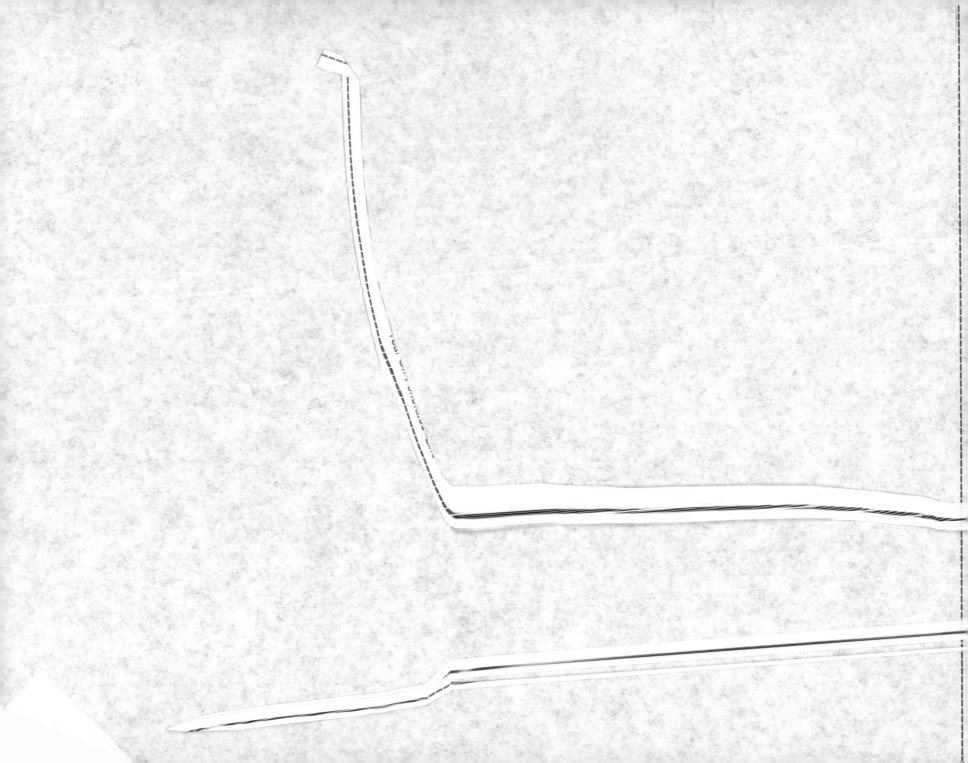

Coelophysis
(see-lo-FISE-iss)

Means "Hollow Form" and refers to its hollow bones.

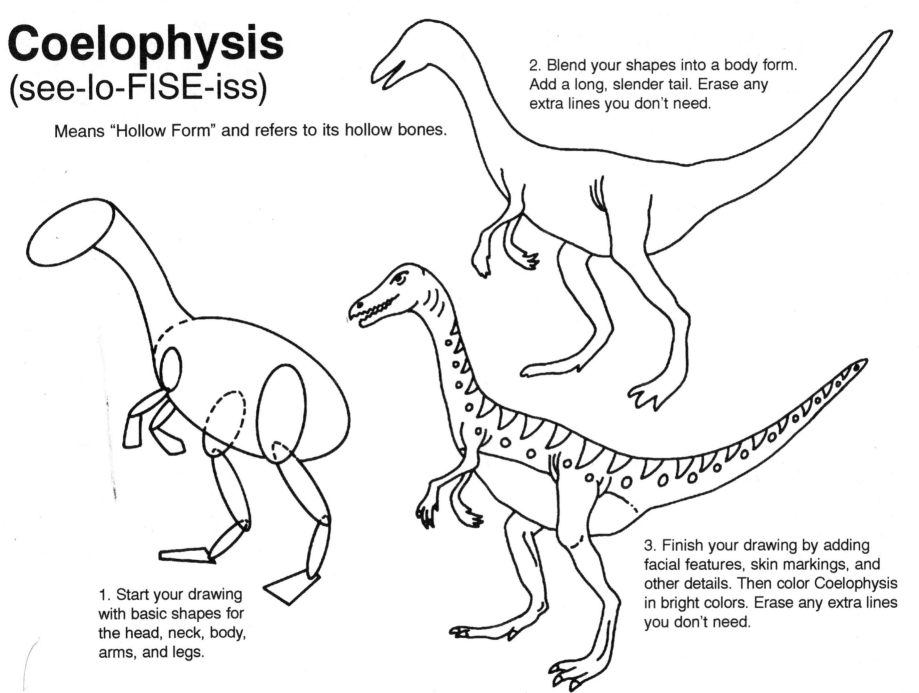

2. Blend your shapes into a body form. Add a long, slender tail. Erase any extra lines you don't need.

1. Start your drawing with basic shapes for the head, neck, body, arms, and legs.

3. Finish your drawing by adding facial features, skin markings, and other details. Then color Coelophysis in bright colors. Erase any extra lines you don't need.

33

Oviraptor (o-vee-RAP-tor)

Means "Egg Stealer" because its fossilized bones were found near another dinosaur's nest of eggs.

The shape of Oviraptor's head tells us that it probably used its deep beak and two sharp teeth to break an eggshell. And its eyes, far apart from each other, could warn the dinosaur of danger while it fed.

Remember: Keep all your lines and shapes lightly drawn.

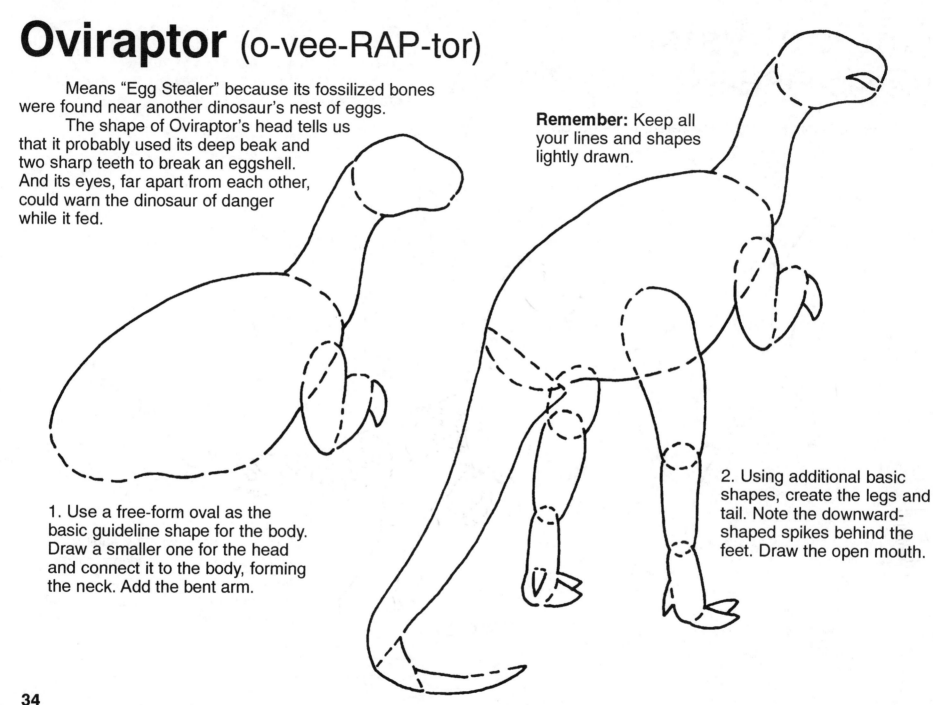

1. Use a free-form oval as the basic guideline shape for the body. Draw a smaller one for the head and connect it to the body, forming the neck. Add the bent arm.

2. Using additional basic shapes, create the legs and tail. Note the downward-shaped spikes behind the feet. Draw the open mouth.

3. Add an eye, a nostril, and a tiny hole at the jaw. Connect and blend all the lines into a smooth body shape. Erase unneeded lines as you go along.

4. Shading and skin texture will give your Oviraptor a dramatic effect.

Tylosaurus
(TYE-lo-sawr-us)

Not a dinosaur, Tylosaurus is one of the largest known seagoing lizards. Close in appearance to a modern crocodile, it was a hunter of fish and shellfish.

1. Carefully draw the basic body shape. Add a small circle for the head and two triangle shapes for the huge mouth. Next, add four ovals for the flippers, attaching them to the body with connector lines.

2. Add the long, curving tail. Then, use basic oval shapes to create the row of back scales.

Remember: Practice makes perfect. Keep drawing and erasing until you are satisfied with the way your picture looks.

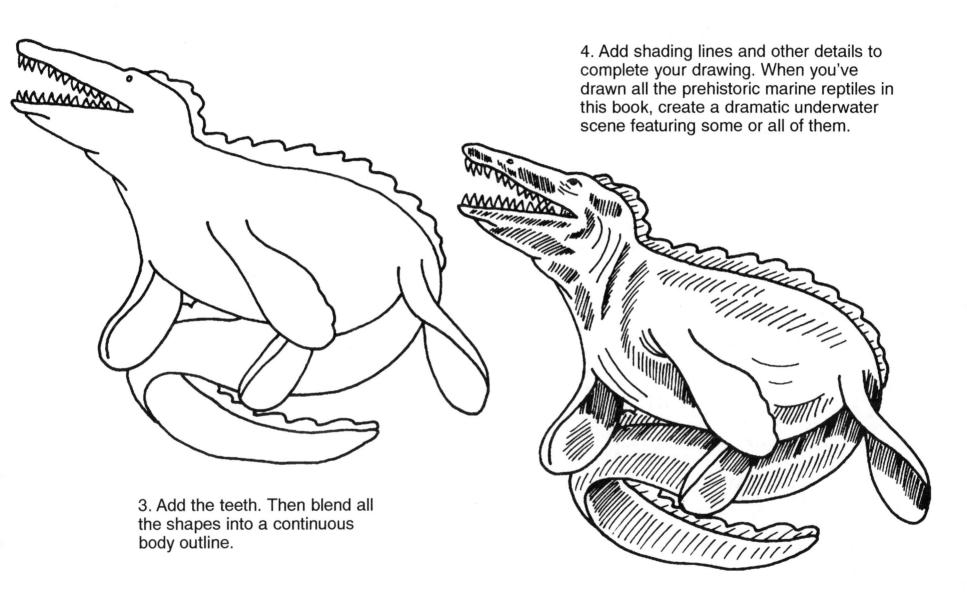

4. Add shading lines and other details to complete your drawing. When you've drawn all the prehistoric marine reptiles in this book, create a dramatic underwater scene featuring some or all of them.

3. Add the teeth. Then blend all the shapes into a continuous body outline.

Lambeosaurus
(LAM-be-uh-sawr-us)

Means "Lambe's Lizard" after Lawrence Lambe, who studied dinosaur fossils.

Lambeosaurus was a crested duckbill dinosaur. It had hollow crests on its head that may have been used to make loud noises.

2. Carefully add the crest on top of the head with a rectangle and a small oval. Then, using basic guideline shapes, lightly draw the arms, hands, legs, feet, and tail.

1. Start by sketching a large oval for the body, and a circle and triangle for the head. Connect the two ovals.

3. And the eye, nostril, and mouth. Blend the guideline shapes into a smooth outline of the dinosaur's body. Erase any lines you no longer need.

4. Add shading, texture, and other finishing touches to complete your Lambeosaurus.

39

Allosaurus
(AL-uh-sawr-us)

Means "Different Lizard" because its spine bones were different from other dinosaurs.

Allosaurus was a big, 40-foot long, meat eating dinosaur. It was quite active for its size.

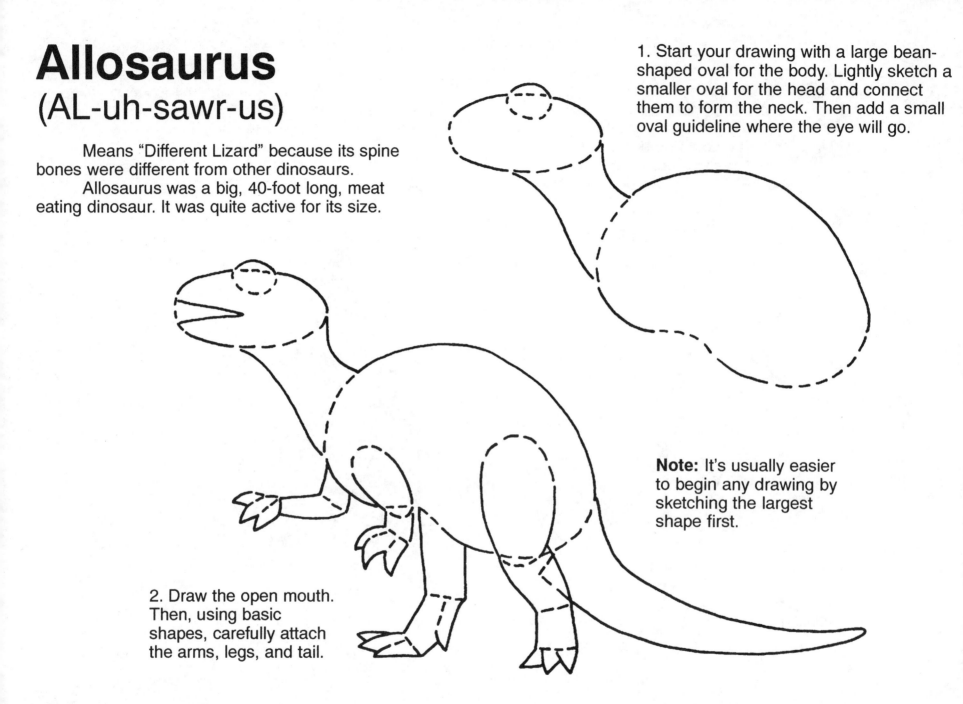

1. Start your drawing with a large bean-shaped oval for the body. Lightly sketch a smaller oval for the head and connect them to form the neck. Then add a small oval guideline where the eye will go.

Note: It's usually easier to begin any drawing by sketching the largest shape first.

2. Draw the open mouth. Then, using basic shapes, carefully attach the arms, legs, and tail.

3. Add the teeth and eye. Then blend the lines and shapes into a smooth, clean outline. Erase any guidelines you no longer need.

4. Finish Allosaurus by adding lots of detail. Shading, bumpy skin textures, and wrinkles will add a realistic look to your drawing. And don't forget some background scenery.

Chasmosaurus
(KAZ-muh-sawr-us)

Means "Opening Lizard" because of the openings in its head frill. The large holes lightened the bony frill's weight.

A plant eater, Chasmosaurus was one of the most widespread dinosaurs. Many have been found in Texas and Alberta, Canada.

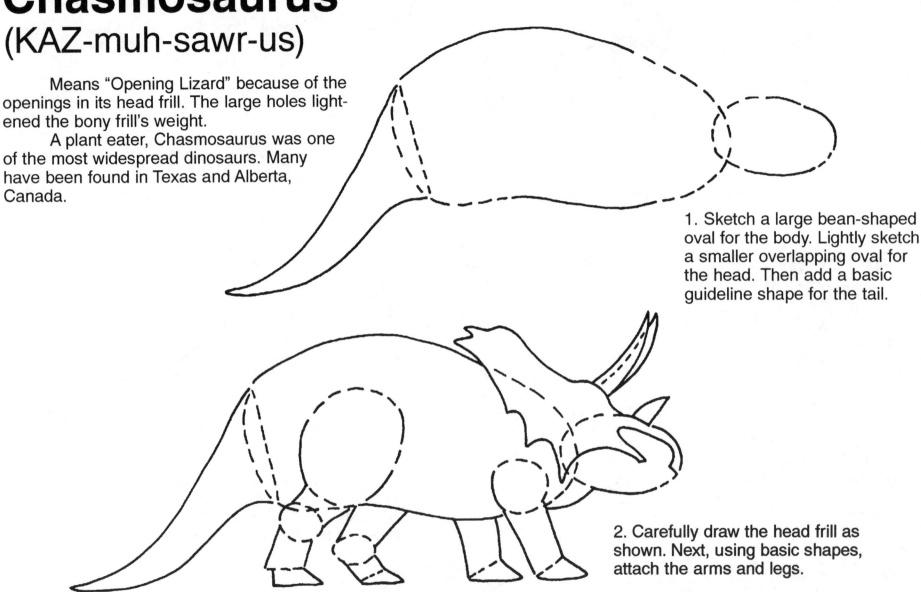

1. Sketch a large bean-shaped oval for the body. Lightly sketch a smaller overlapping oval for the head. Then add a basic guideline shape for the tail.

2. Carefully draw the head frill as shown. Next, using basic shapes, attach the arms and legs.

3. Add an eye, then create the open mouth and nostril. Next, add two over-lapping horns on the frill, and a smaller horn on the front of the head. Blend the shapes into a smooth, clean outline. Erase any unneeded guidelines.

4. Finish Chasmosaurus by adding lots of shading and detail. Now this dinosaur is ready to go hunting for some food!

Stenonychosaurus
(sten-ON-ik-uh-sawr-us)

Means "Narrow-Clawed Lizard" because of the sharp, upturned claw on each foot.

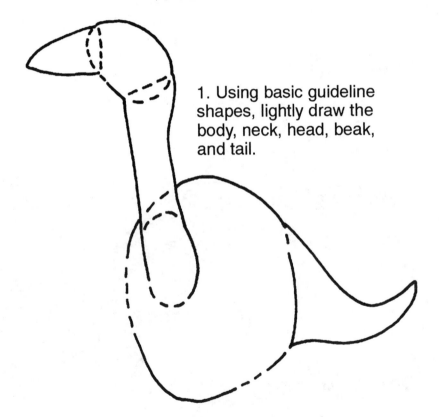

1. Using basic guideline shapes, lightly draw the body, neck, head, beak, and tail.

2. Attach basic shapes for the arms, hands, legs, and feet. Then create the beak.

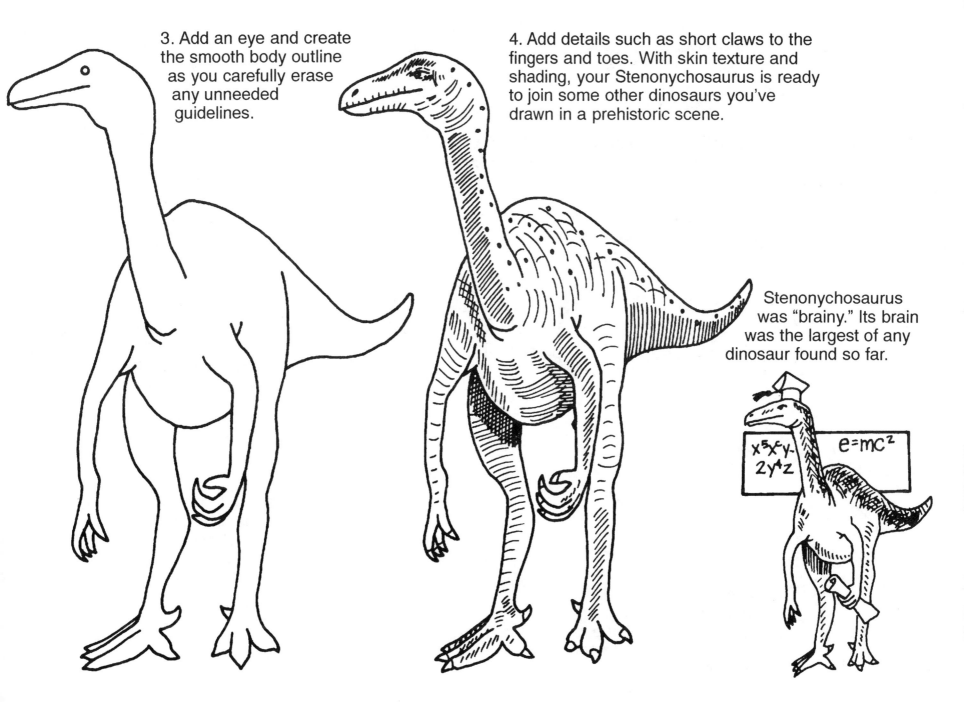

3. Add an eye and create the smooth body outline as you carefully erase any unneeded guidelines.

4. Add details such as short claws to the fingers and toes. With skin texture and shading, your Stenonychosaurus is ready to join some other dinosaurs you've drawn in a prehistoric scene.

Stenonychosaurus was "brainy." Its brain was the largest of any dinosaur found so far.

$x^5x^-y-2y^4z$

$e=mc^2$

Archaeopteryx
(ar-kee-OP-ter-ix)

Means "Ancient Wing" because many believe it to be one of the first birds. Fossils formed in limestone in Germany show impressions of long feathers on the wings and tail.

1. Draw an oval for the body and a small circle for the head. Connect them to form the neck. Then add two overlapping triangles for the beak.

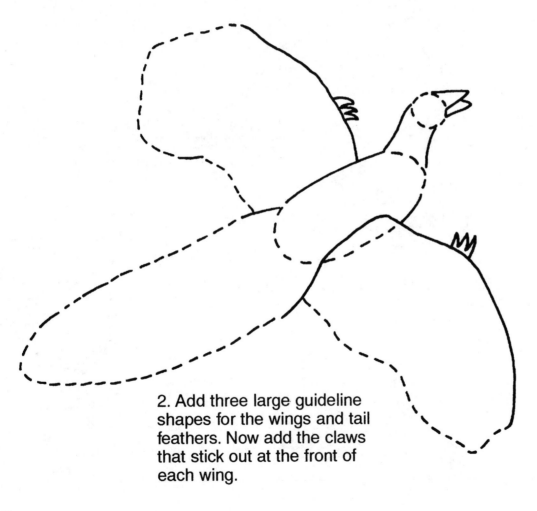

2. Add three large guideline shapes for the wings and tail feathers. Now add the claws that stick out at the front of each wing.

Note: Guidelines should always be lightly drawn. If you don't like the way something looks, erase and try again.

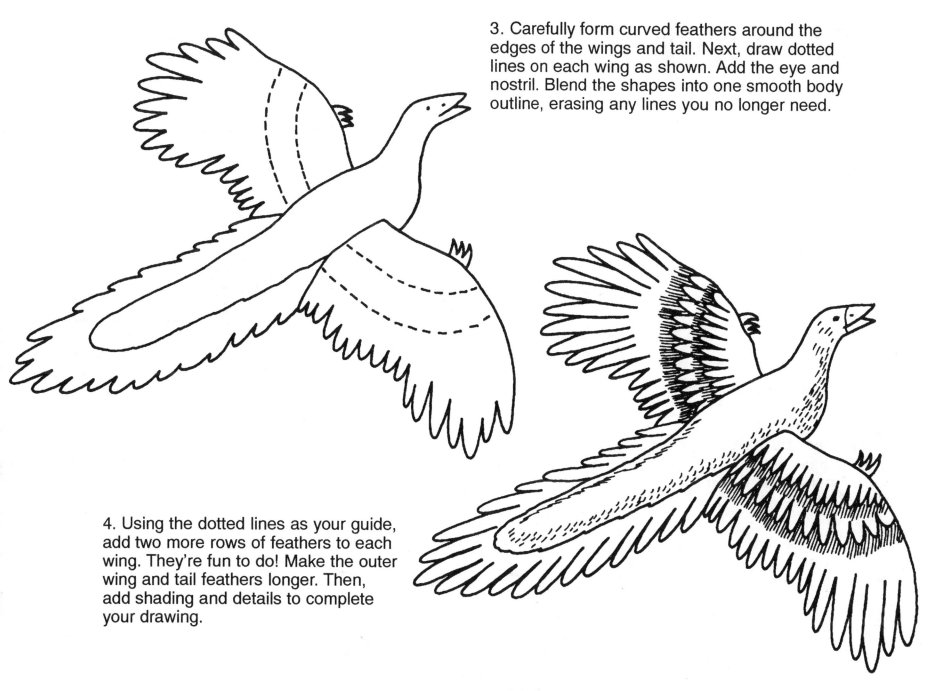

3. Carefully form curved feathers around the edges of the wings and tail. Next, draw dotted lines on each wing as shown. Add the eye and nostril. Blend the shapes into one smooth body outline, erasing any lines you no longer need.

4. Using the dotted lines as your guide, add two more rows of feathers to each wing. They're fun to do! Make the outer wing and tail feathers longer. Then, add shading and details to complete your drawing.

Nodosaurus
(no-doe-SAWR-us)

Means "Toothless Lizard" because it was thought to be toothless.

Nodosaurus is one of the earliest known armored dinosaurs. Fossils have been found in New Jersey, Alabama, Kansas, and Wyoming.

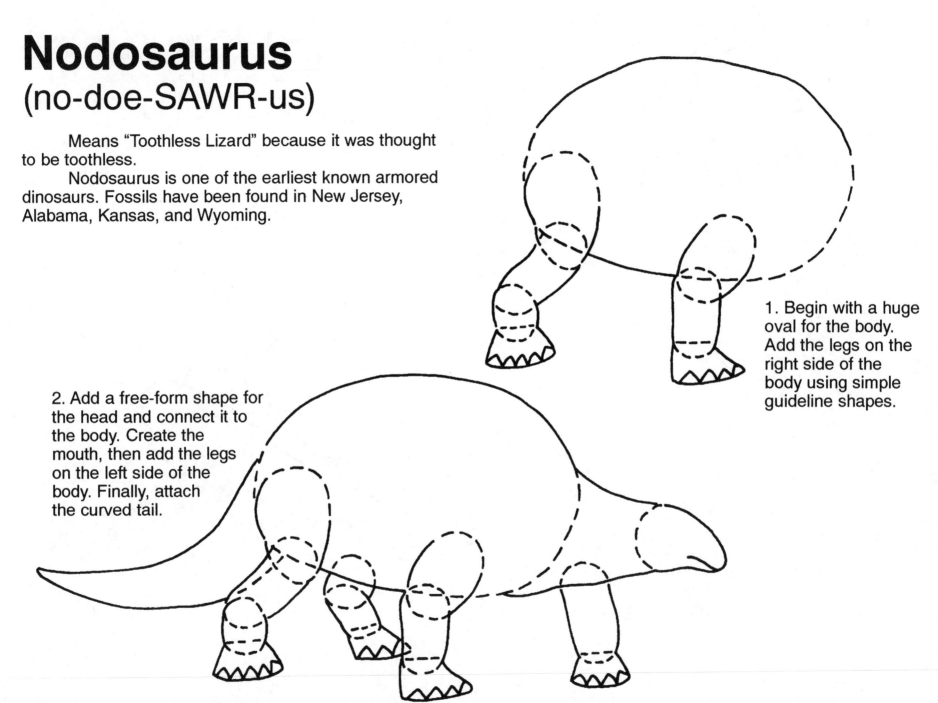

1. Begin with a huge oval for the body. Add the legs on the right side of the body using simple guideline shapes.

2. Add a free-form shape for the head and connect it to the body. Create the mouth, then add the legs on the left side of the body. Finally, attach the curved tail.

3. Add the eye and nostril, then blend the shapes together into a smooth body outline. Note that the line forming the back is rippled or bumpy. Erase any lines you no longer need.

4. Add vertical and horizontal lines on the neck and back to form rough little squares. Add small oval shapes within the squares to show Nodosaurus's armor plating. Complete the eye and add more shading lines and texture.

Ouranosaurus
(our-AHN-uh-SAWR-us)

Means "Valiant Lizard," after a West African word for "fearless." A relative of Iguanodon, Ouranosaurus had a sail on its back, probably to keep it from overheating in its homeland of Africa.

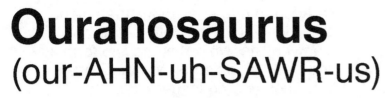

1. Start with a large free-form oval for the body. Add the head and pointed "beak," then connect them to the body. Next, use simple shapes to draw the arms and legs.

2. Attach a long curvy tail. Next, create the sail by sketching a line from behind the head to halfway down the tail. Add oval shapes to the sail as shown.

Note: Steps 1 and 2 establish the overall structure and look of your drawing. In steps 3 and 4 you are simply refining and adding details.

3. Add an eye and blend the guideline shapes together. Erase unneeded lines as you go along.

4. When you're satisfied with the way your Ouranosaurus looks, add shading lines or color the dinosaur with your choice of colors.

Brachiosaurus
(BRAK-ee-uh-SAWR-us)

Means "Arm Lizard" due to its long front legs.
The tiny head of Brachiosaurus had huge nostrils on top. They may have helped to keep the dinosaur cool.

1. Lightly sketch the basic guideline shapes—ovals, rectangles, and triangles—for the body and legs.

2. High above the body draw the head, using a small oval and a circle. Connect the head to the body with two long curved lines. Then add the tail.

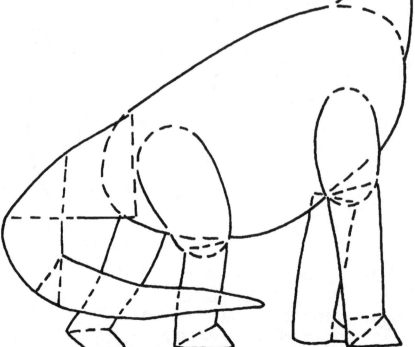

3. Add the mouth and eye. Blend the shapes into a continuous smooth outline, erasing unnecessary guidelines as you go along.

4. Lots of interesting shading will make Brachiosaurus come alive. What color do you think this dinosaur was?

Psittacosaurus
(SIT-uh-ko-sawr-us)

Means "Parrot Lizard" because of its parrot-shaped head.
Scientists think that Psittacosaurus belonged to a group of dinosaurs that evolved into the big-horned dinosaurs, such as Triceratops.

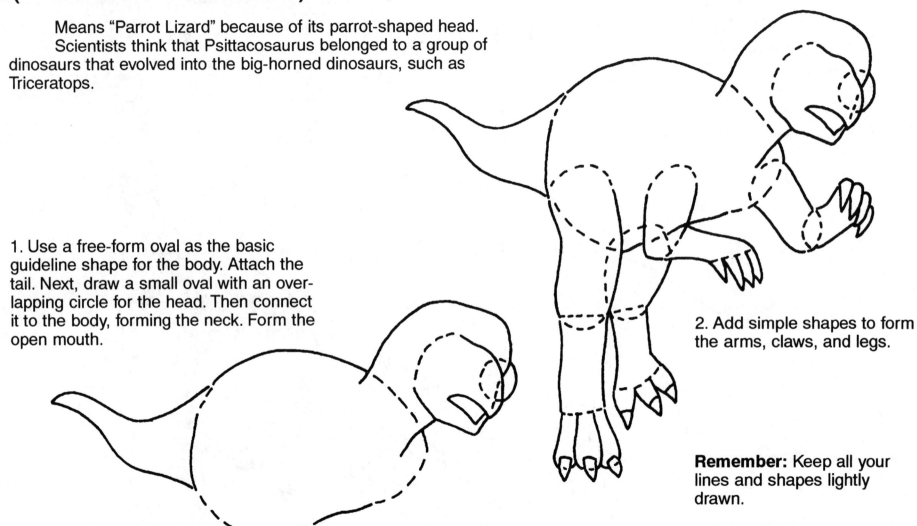

1. Use a free-form oval as the basic guideline shape for the body. Attach the tail. Next, draw a small oval with an overlapping circle for the head. Then connect it to the body, forming the neck. Form the open mouth.

2. Add simple shapes to form the arms, claws, and legs.

Remember: Keep all your lines and shapes lightly drawn.

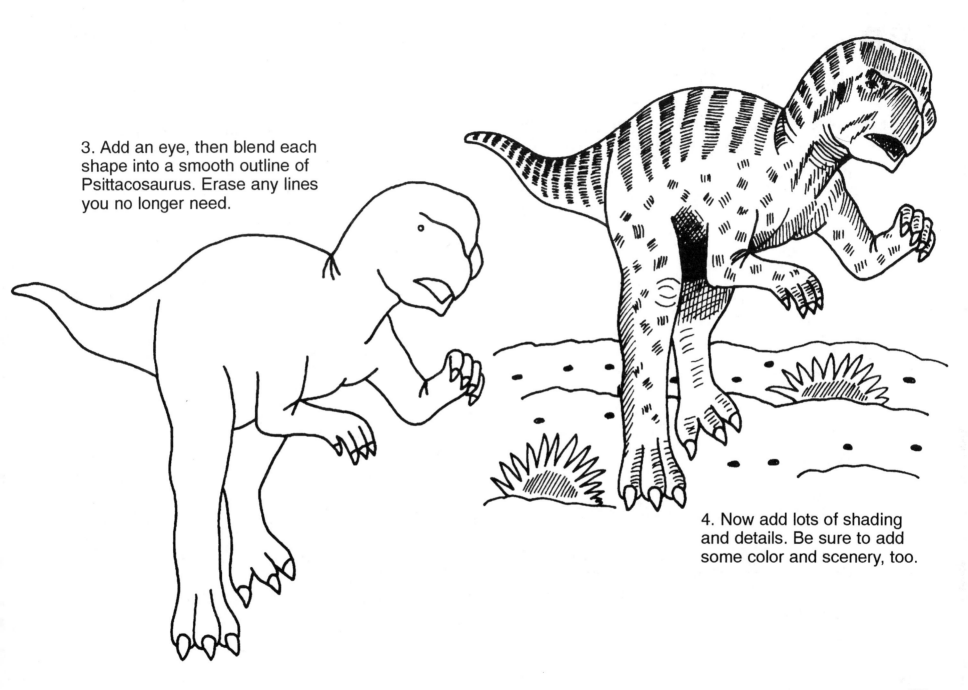

3. Add an eye, then blend each shape into a smooth outline of Psittacosaurus. Erase any lines you no longer need.

4. Now add lots of shading and details. Be sure to add some color and scenery, too.

Dinichthys
(die-NIK-thees)

Means "Terrible Fish," and it must have been. Instead of teeth, this 30-foot-long sea relative of the dinosaurs had huge fangs made of bone.

2. Add the eye circles. Make the tail longer, adding wavy fins to the outside edges. Then, carefully create the open mouth with two jagged lines. Finally, add two small fins on the body, as shown.

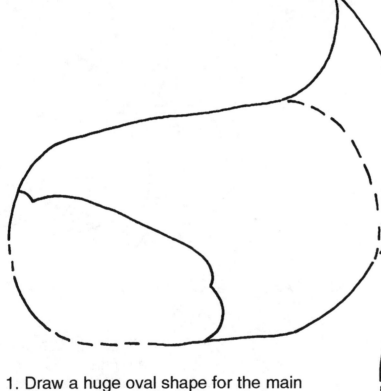

1. Draw a huge oval shape for the main part of the body. Then attach a short, curved shape for the beginning of the tail. Add a rounded line for the mouth area.

3. To give the mouth dimension, add more jagged lines as shown. Then add the the body lines as you blend the shapes together.

4. Add lots of interesting details and shading. Now Dinichthys is ready to join the other terrors of the prehistoric seas.

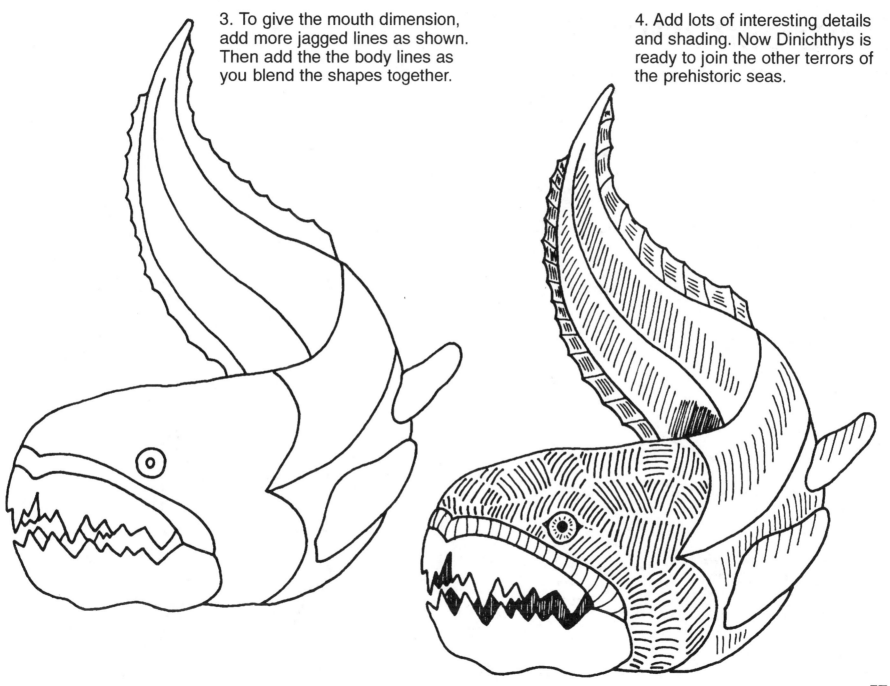

Fabrosaurus
(FAB-ruh-sawr-us)

Means "Fabre's Lizard"-named after Jean Fabre, a French scientist.

1. Lightly sketch a large, free-form oval for the body and a smaller oval for the head. Connect the two ovals and add the tail.

2. Using more basic shapes, add the short arms, the legs, and the mouth.

Note: It's usually easier to begin any drawing by sketching the largest shape first.

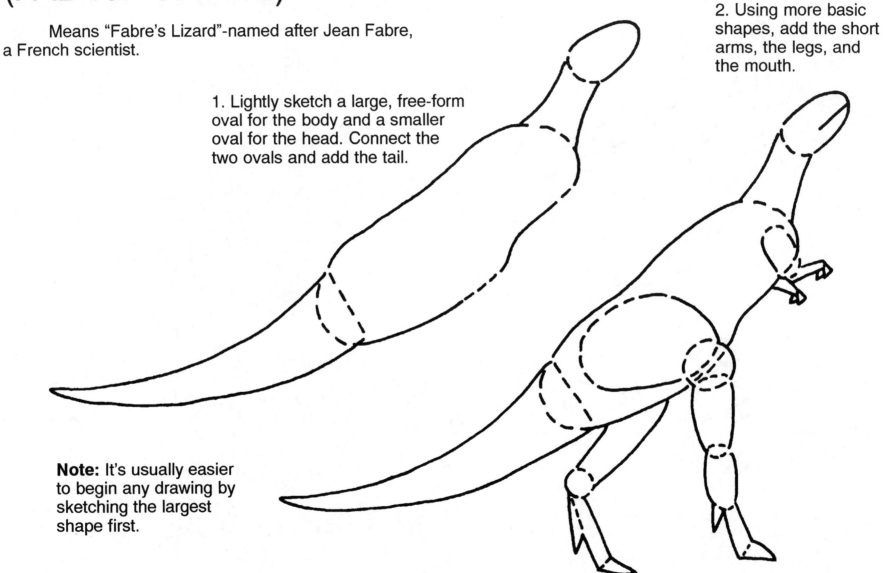

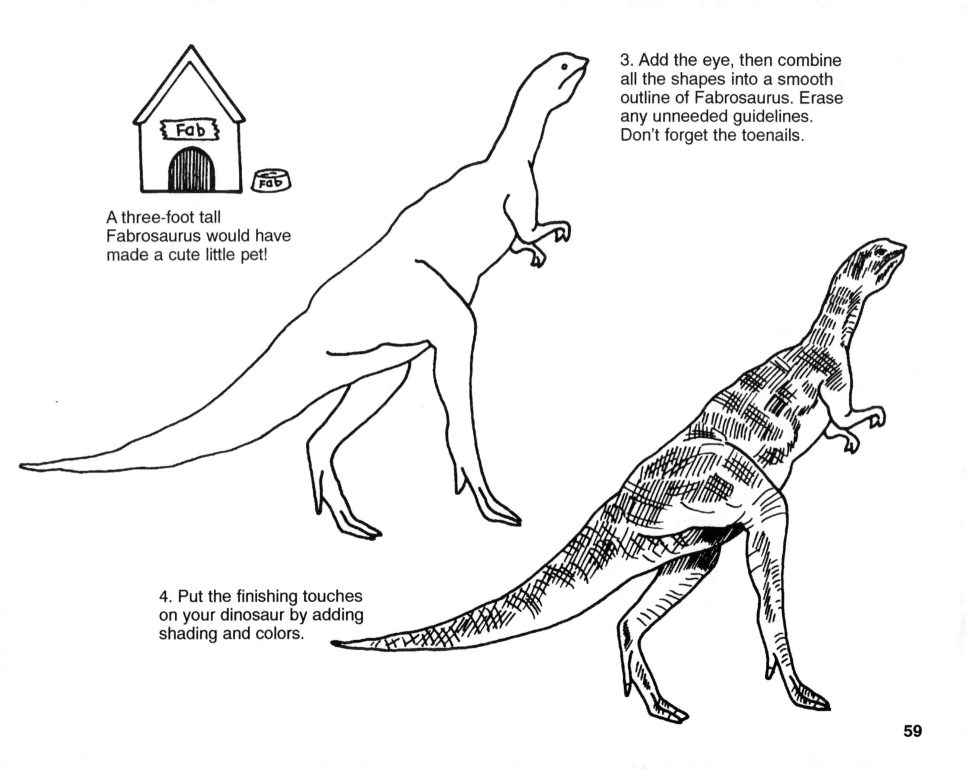

A three-foot tall Fabrosaurus would have made a cute little pet!

3. Add the eye, then combine all the shapes into a smooth outline of Fabrosaurus. Erase any unneeded guidelines. Don't forget the toenails.

4. Put the finishing touches on your dinosaur by adding shading and colors.

Heterodontosaurus
(het-er-uh-DON-tuh-sawr-us)

Means "Different Teeth Lizard" because it had three different kinds of teeth.

1. Start by sketching oval guideline shapes for the body, head, and snout. Connect the head to the body with two short lines. Add more basic shapes to create the arms.

Remember: It's easy to draw almost anything if you first break it down into simple shapes.

2. Add the open mouth. Next, draw the legs, feet, and tail.

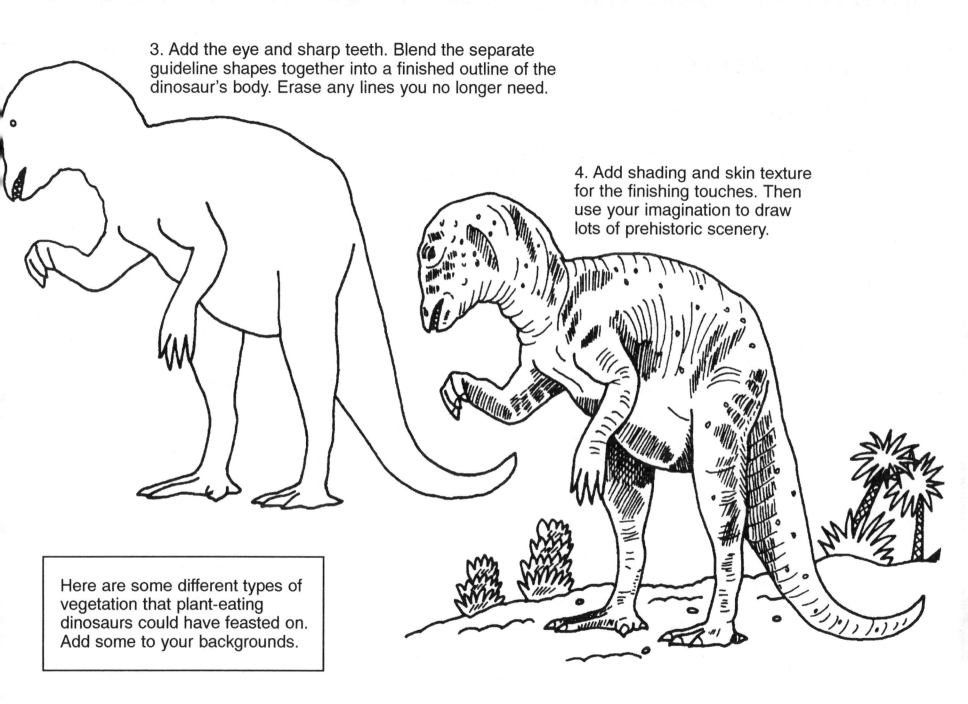

3. Add the eye and sharp teeth. Blend the separate guideline shapes together into a finished outline of the dinosaur's body. Erase any lines you no longer need.

4. Add shading and skin texture for the finishing touches. Then use your imagination to draw lots of prehistoric scenery.

Here are some different types of vegetation that plant-eating dinosaurs could have feasted on. Add some to your backgrounds.

Tarbosaurus
(TAR-bo-sawr-us)

Means "Terrible Lizard" because this meat-eater's powerful body and dagger-like teeth must have struck fear into smaller dinosaurs.

This enormous dinosaur is known from ten complete skeletons found in the Gobi Desert of Mongolia.

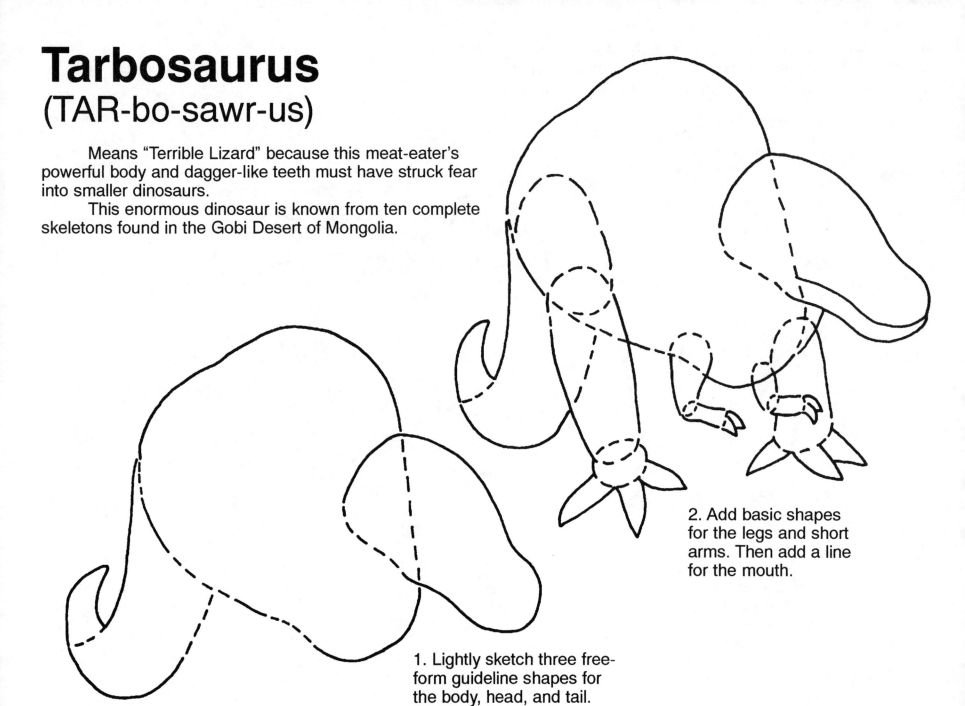

2. Add basic shapes for the legs and short arms. Then add a line for the mouth.

1. Lightly sketch three free-form guideline shapes for the body, head, and tail.

4. Add shading, skin texture, and other details to complete your drawing of terrible Tarbosaurus!

3. Add an eye, nostrils, and a tiny hole at the back of the head. Then blend the shapes together.

Remember: Practice makes perfect. Keep drawing and erasing until you are satisfied with the way your picture looks.

Chialingosaurus
(chye-ah-ling-uh-SAWR-us)

Means "Chia-ling Lizard," referring to the Chia-ling River in China, where it was found.

A stegosaur with spikes on its body, Chialingosaurus munched on plants.

1. Begin by drawing a large free-form oval for the body. Attach the head and neck at one end, and the tail at the other.

2. Add the basic guideline shapes for the four legs. Next, carefully draw a double row of triangular plates down the back.

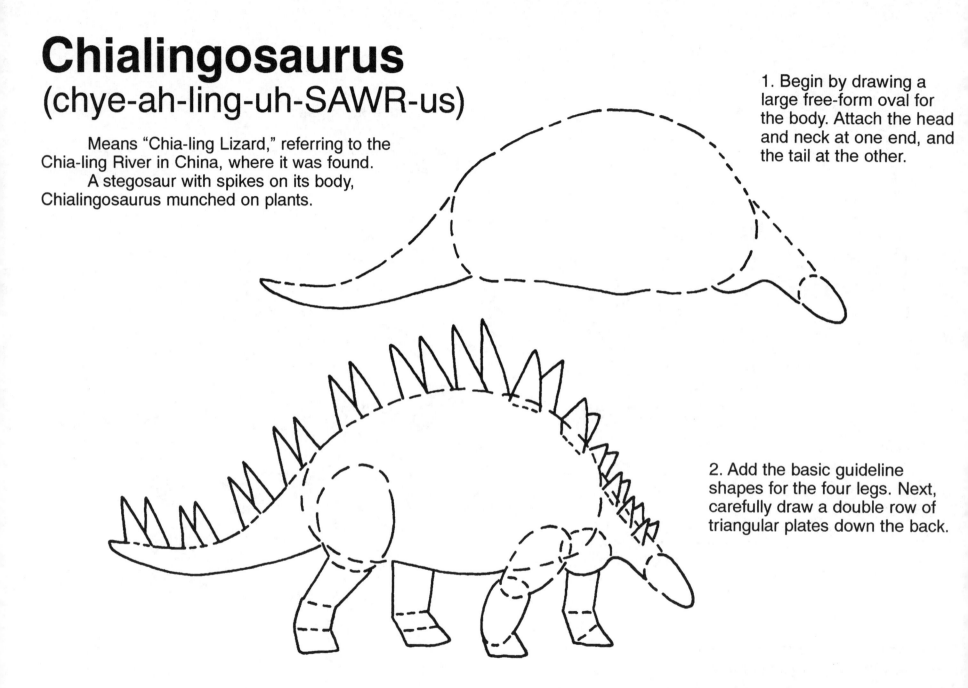

3. Complete the head and combine all the guideline shapes together. Note that the plates closer to the head are shaped differently from those on the middle back and tail.

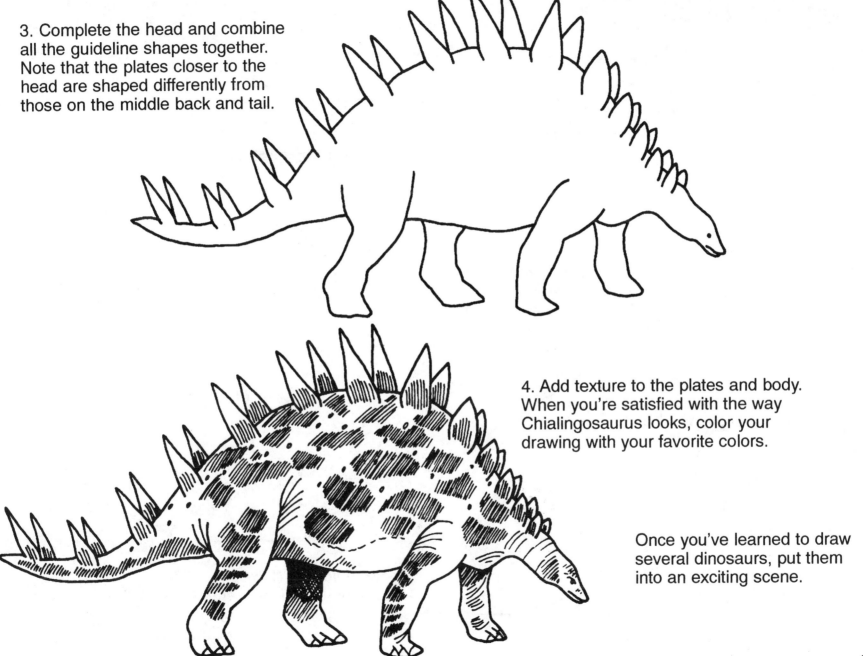

4. Add texture to the plates and body. When you're satisfied with the way Chialingosaurus looks, color your drawing with your favorite colors.

Once you've learned to draw several dinosaurs, put them into an exciting scene.

Megalosaurus
(MEG-uh-lo-sawr-us)

Means "Big Lizard" due to its large size.
Early in the nineteenth century, Megalosaurus
was the first dinosaur to be described and named.

2. Add the basic shapes for
the legs and tail. Then create
the open mouth.

1. Begin by drawing the basic
shapes for the body and head.
Connect the head to the body,
forming the neck. Add more
basic shapes for the
arms and hands.

Note: If you don't like the
way something looks, erase
and try again.

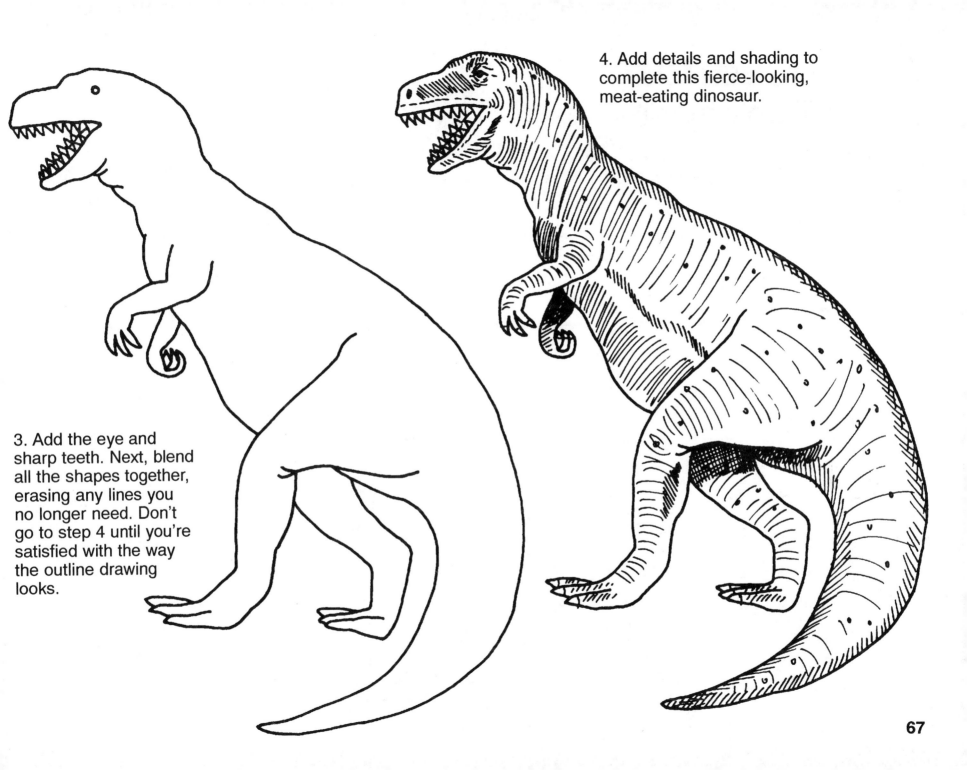

3. Add the eye and sharp teeth. Next, blend all the shapes together, erasing any lines you no longer need. Don't go to step 4 until you're satisfied with the way the outline drawing looks.

4. Add details and shading to complete this fierce-looking, meat-eating dinosaur.

Anatosaurus
(ah-NAT-uh-sawr-us)

Means "Duck Lizard" because of its flat, duck-like bill. Fossil impressions of Anatosaurus show that it had rough, pebbly skin.

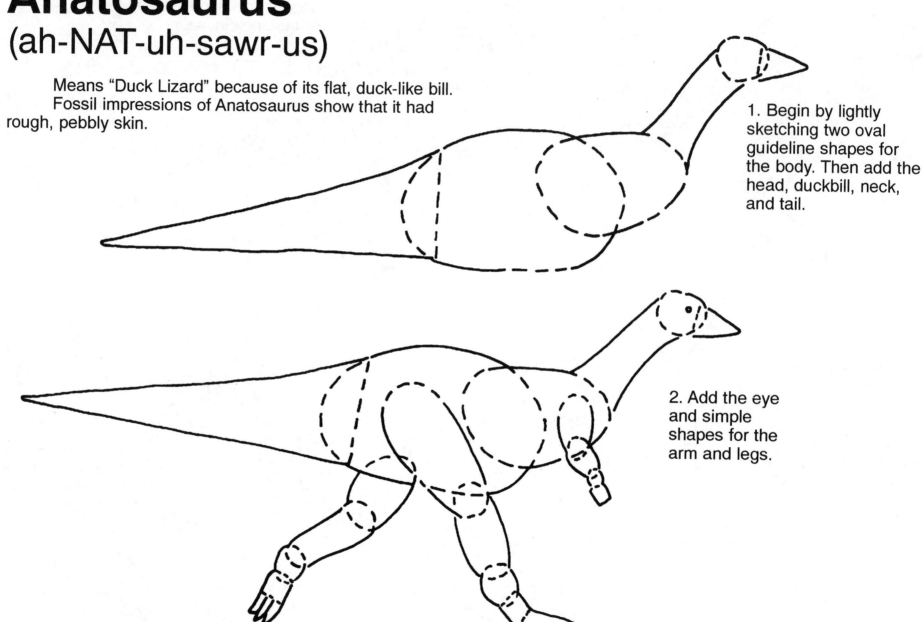

1. Begin by lightly sketching two oval guideline shapes for the body. Then add the head, duckbill, neck, and tail.

2. Add the eye and simple shapes for the arm and legs.

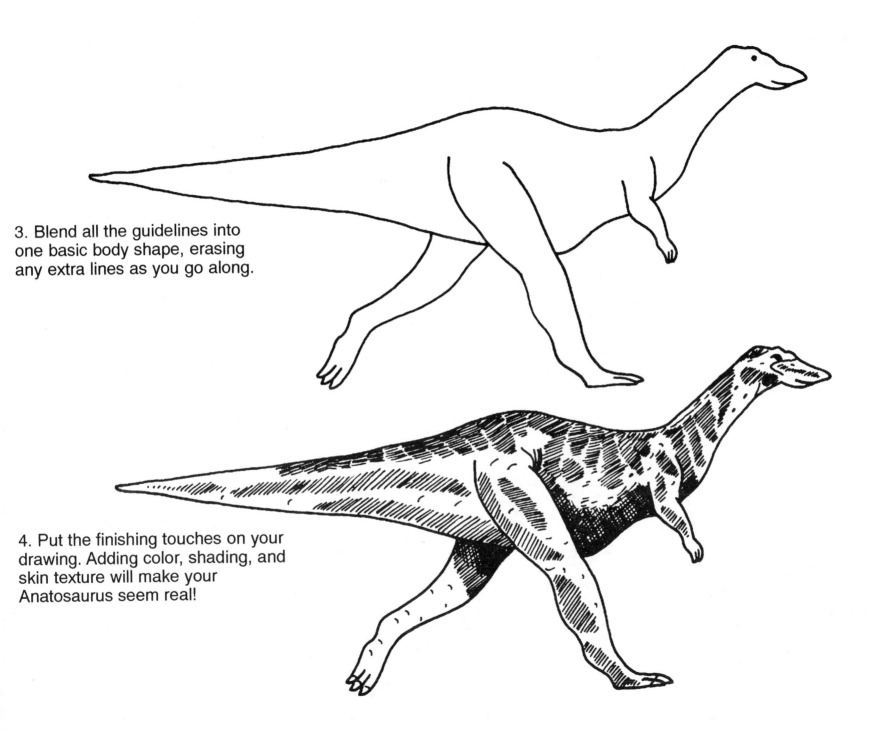

3. Blend all the guidelines into one basic body shape, erasing any extra lines as you go along.

4. Put the finishing touches on your drawing. Adding color, shading, and skin texture will make your Anatosaurus seem real!

Archelon
(AR-kee-lon)

Means "Ruler Tortoise" because, so far, it's the largest turtle that ever lived.

Not a dinosaur, Archelon was a giant turtle that lived in the middle of North America in an inland sea.

1. Draw a large oval for the body. Add the other basic shapes for the head, neck, and tail.

Note: Always draw your guidelines lightly in steps 1 and 2. It will be easier to erase them later.

2. Draw a line across the body for the shell. Then sketch the guideline shapes for the paddle-like flippers.

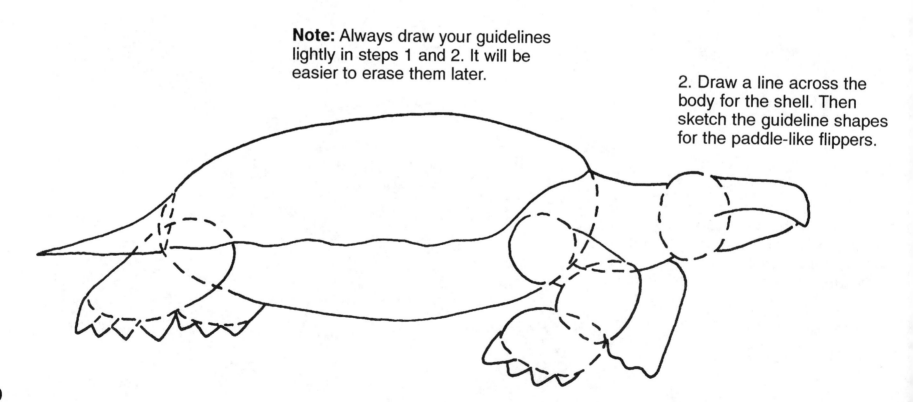

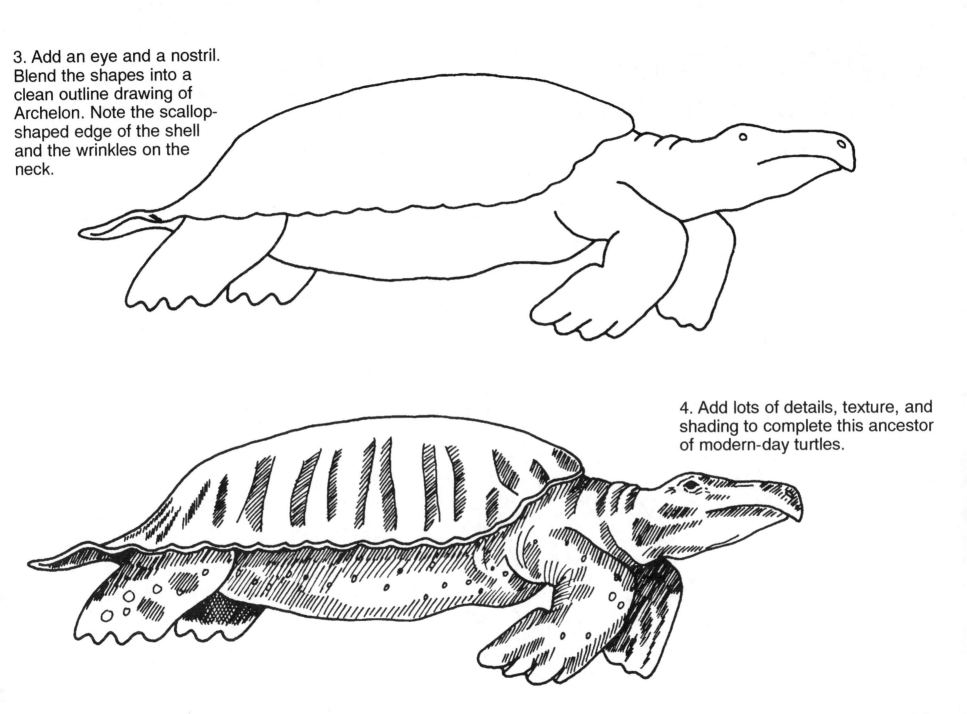

3. Add an eye and a nostril. Blend the shapes into a clean outline drawing of Archelon. Note the scallop-shaped edge of the shell and the wrinkles on the neck.

4. Add lots of details, texture, and shading to complete this ancestor of modern-day turtles.

Leptoceratops
(lep-toe-SAIR-uh-tops)

Means "Slender Horned Face" because of its appearance.

1. Lightly sketch the basic guideline shapes—oval for the body and triangles for the head and tail. Connect the head to the body. Add a small triangle for the beak and a short line for the mouth.

2. Attach the shapes for the arms and legs.

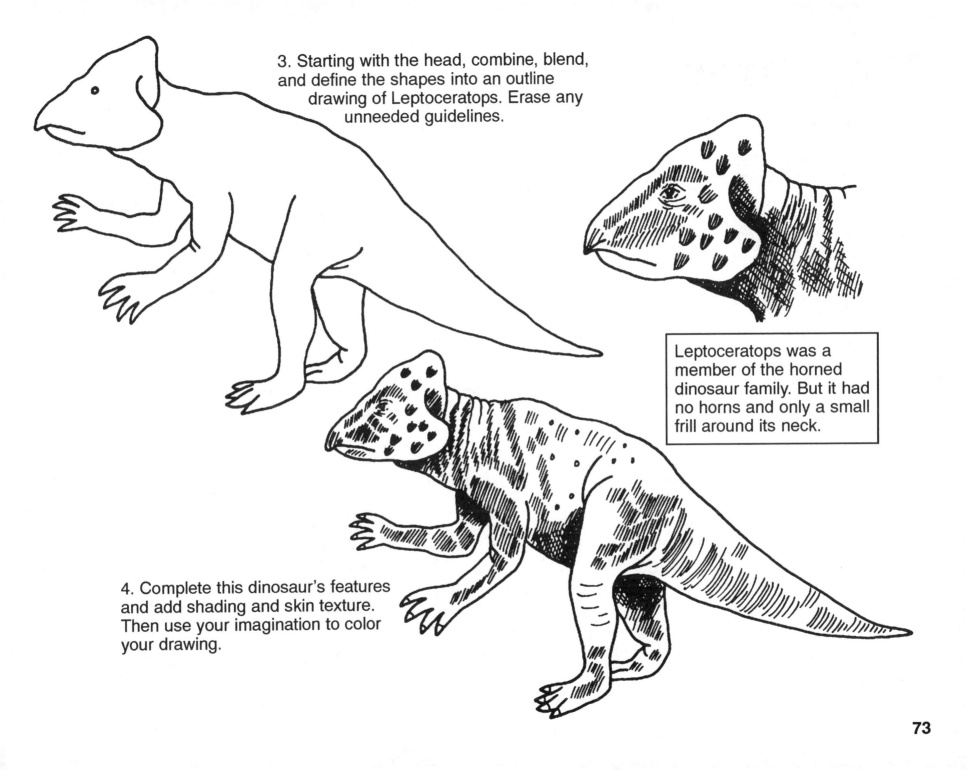

3. Starting with the head, combine, blend, and define the shapes into an outline drawing of Leptoceratops. Erase any unneeded guidelines.

Leptoceratops was a member of the horned dinosaur family. But it had no horns and only a small frill around its neck.

4. Complete this dinosaur's features and add shading and skin texture. Then use your imagination to color your drawing.

73

Dilophosaurus
(dye-LO-fuh-sawr-us)

Means "Two-crested Lizard" because of the two crests on its head. Unlike other big meat-eaters, Dilophosaurus had bone joints that would have allowed it to wrinkle its nose!

1. Start by drawing two free-form ovals-one for the body and one for the head. Connect the ovals and add the tail.

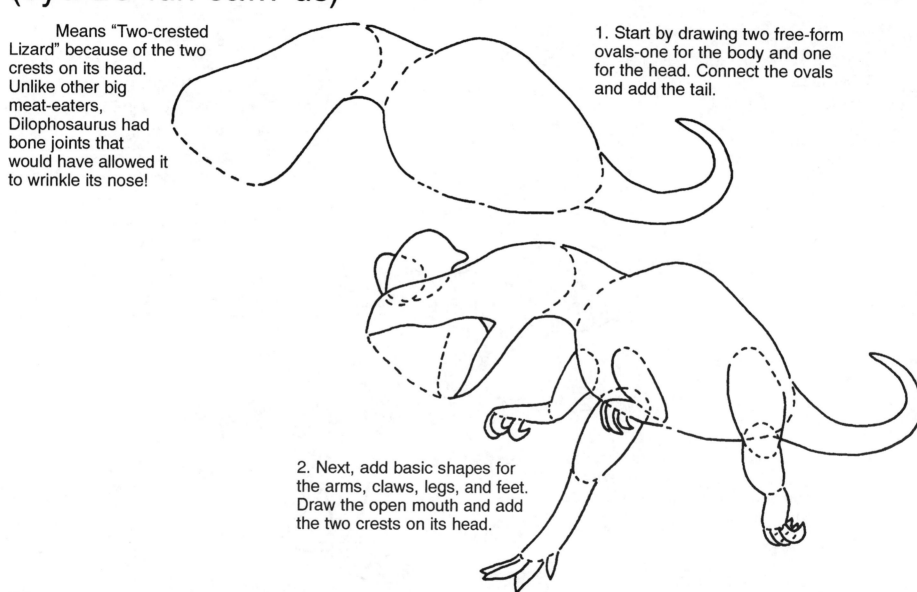

2. Next, add basic shapes for the arms, claws, legs, and feet. Draw the open mouth and add the two crests on its head.

3. Add an eye and a nostril. Blend the lines and shapes into a smooth outline of Dilophosaurus. Then add lots of pointy teeth.

Remember: Practice makes perfect. Keep drawing and erasing until you are satisfied with the way your picture looks.

4. Now add the final touches. Spots, shading, and skin wrinkles will make this dinosaur look ferociously real!

Rhamphorhynchus
(ram-fo-RINK-us)

Means "Prow Beak" because its beak was curved.
Not a dinosaur, Rhamphorhynchus was a flying fish-eater, just like our modern seagull!

2. Carefully add the huge wings and curved tail. Note the small triangles on the tip of the tail.

1. Lightly sketch the oval body and head. Connect the two basic shapes to form the neck. Add the triangle shapes for the big open beak. Carefully form each section of the arms, hands, legs, and feet. Note how the shapes fit together.

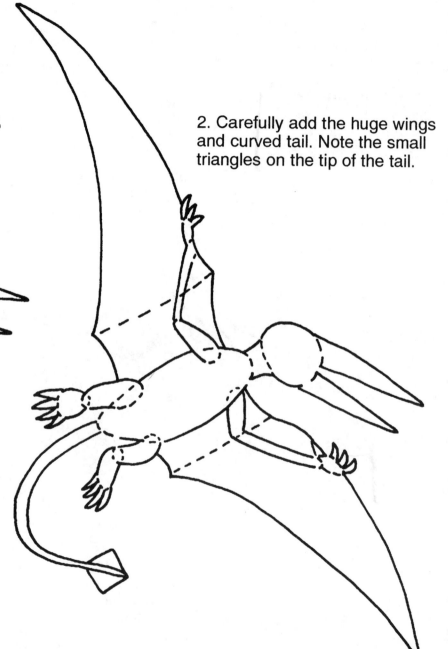

Note: This drawing may seem a bit complicated. However, if you break each step down into smaller steps, and follow along carefully, you'll be amazed at how easy they really are.

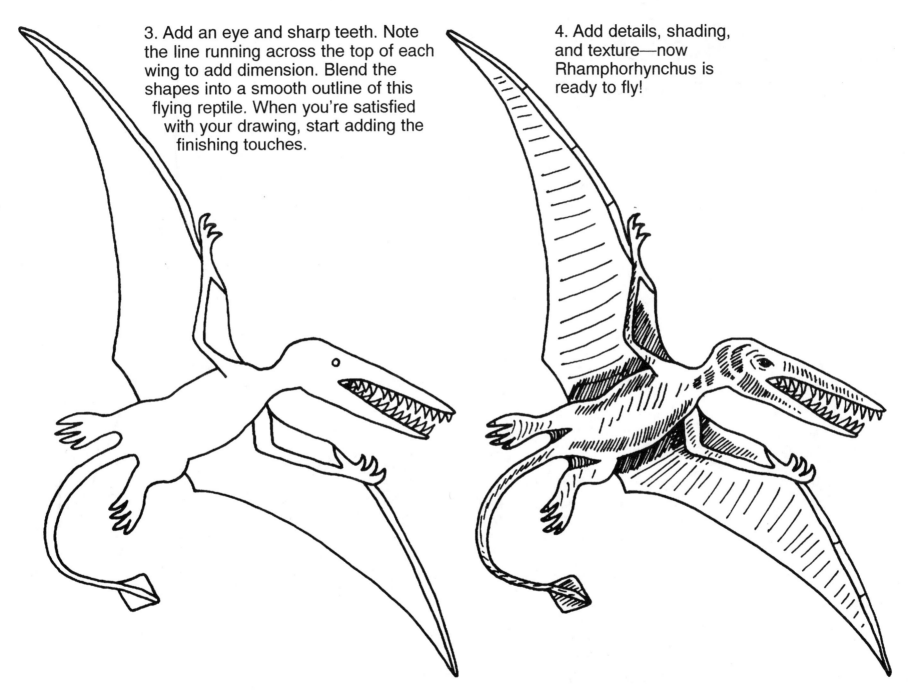

3. Add an eye and sharp teeth. Note the line running across the top of each wing to add dimension. Blend the shapes into a smooth outline of this flying reptile. When you're satisfied with your drawing, start adding the finishing touches.

4. Add details, shading, and texture—now Rhamphorhynchus is ready to fly!

Hylaeosaurus
(hy-LAY-ee-uh-sawr-us)

Means "Wood Lizard" because of the place in England where it was found.

Armored Hylaeosaurus lived near Wealden Lake, a body of water that formed as the continents drifted apart during the early Cretaceous period.

1. Draw a free-form oval as the basic guideline shape for the body. Draw a smaller overlapping oval for the head. Add more simple shapes for the legs, feet, and tail.

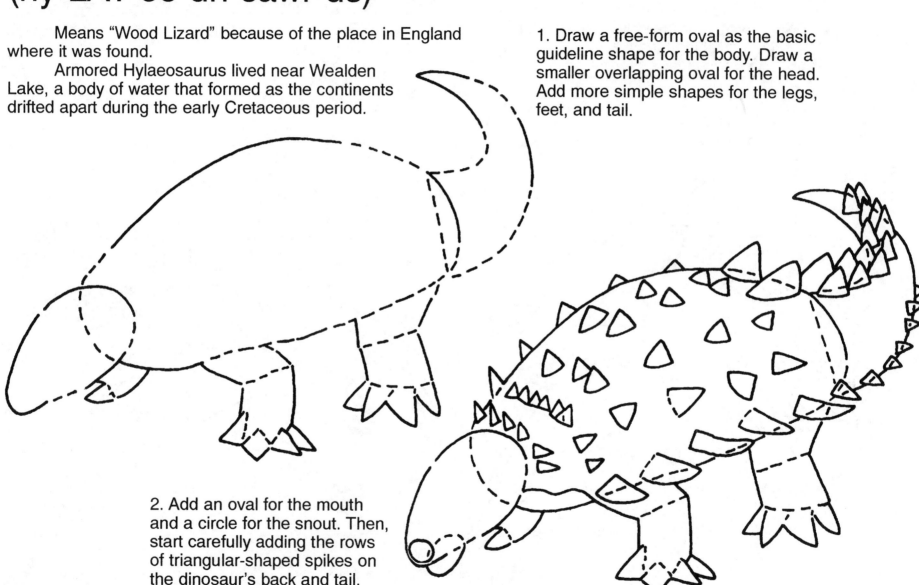

2. Add an oval for the mouth and a circle for the snout. Then, start carefully adding the rows of triangular-shaped spikes on the dinosaur's back and tail.

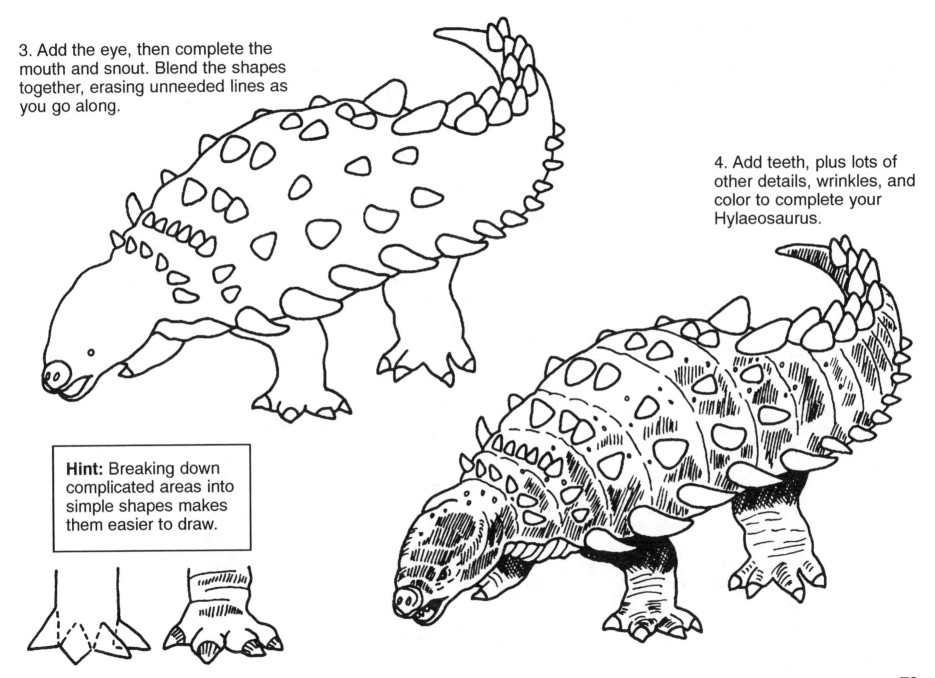

3. Add the eye, then complete the mouth and snout. Blend the shapes together, erasing unneeded lines as you go along.

4. Add teeth, plus lots of other details, wrinkles, and color to complete your Hylaeosaurus.

Hint: Breaking down complicated areas into simple shapes makes them easier to draw.

Deinonychus
(dyne-ON-ik-us)

Means "Terrible Claw" because of the giant, curved claw on top of each foot.

Wolf-sized Deinonychus, a meat-eater, may have hunted in packs.

1. Draw a large oval for the body and a smaller oval for the head. Connect the two ovals to form the neck. Then attach a long triangle for the tail.

2. Create the mouth. Then, using simple guideline shapes, sketch the arms, legs, and claws. Note the giant, curved claw on top of this dinosaur's feet.

Remember: Keep all your lines lightly drawn. It will be easier to erase them later.

3. Add the eye, nostril, and sharp teeth. Starting with the head, blend the shapes into an outline drawing of this fierce, meat-eating dinosaur. Keep drawing, erasing, and re-drawing until you are satisfied.

4. Add some exciting finishing touches. Shading, skin texture, and color will make Deinonychus come alive!

Metriorhynchus
(met-ree-oh-RING-kus)

Means "Long Snout"—just take a look and you'll see why!
An ancestor of the modern crocodile, Metriorhynchus was not a dinosaur but a prehistoric aquatic reptile. Notice its strange dolphinlike tail!

1. Begin your drawing with a long, free-form oval for the body. Add two triangles for the head and another for the tail. Connect the head to the body as shown.

2. Add the basic shapes for the eye and flippers. Then add the rows of menacing teeth.

Note: It's usually easier to begin any drawing by sketching the largest shape first.

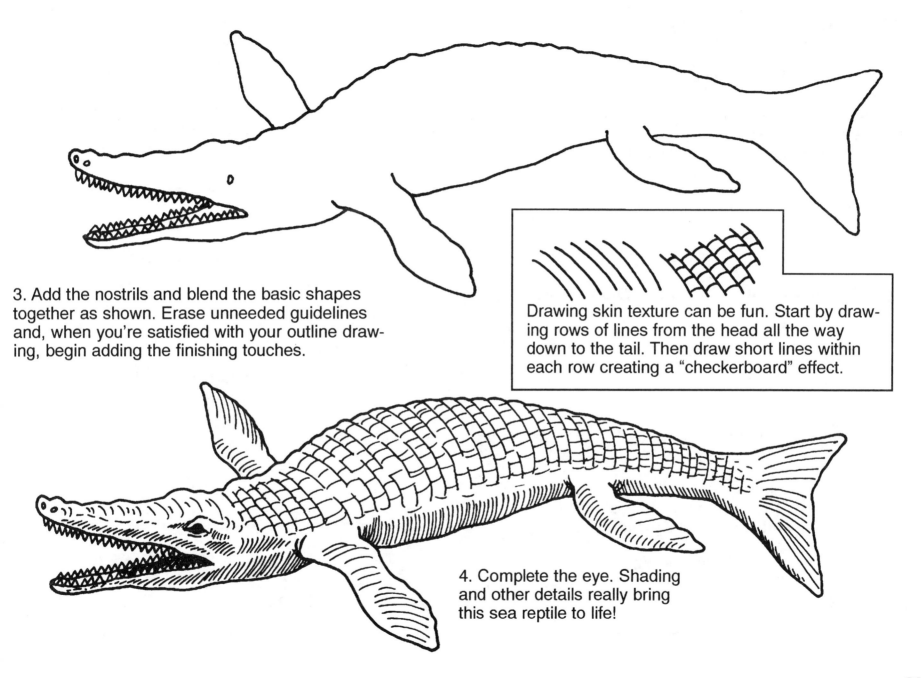

3. Add the nostrils and blend the basic shapes together as shown. Erase unneeded guidelines and, when you're satisfied with your outline drawing, begin adding the finishing touches.

Drawing skin texture can be fun. Start by drawing rows of lines from the head all the way down to the tail. Then draw short lines within each row creating a "checkerboard" effect.

4. Complete the eye. Shading and other details really bring this sea reptile to life!

Dimetrodon
(dye-MET-ruh-don)

Means "Two-Measure Teeth" because it had teeth of two different sizes.

Dimetrodon was not a dinosaur, but a Pelycosaur, an ancestor of the mammal-like reptiles.

1. Lightly sketch two overlapping ovals for the body and head, as shown. Add the triangle-shaped tail.

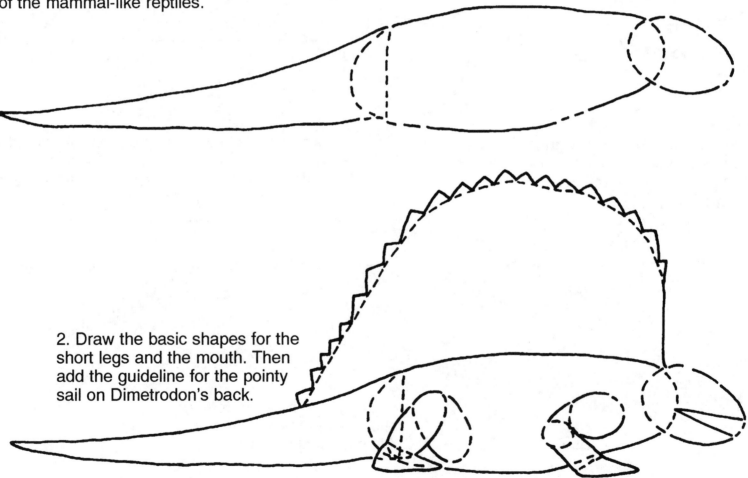

2. Draw the basic shapes for the short legs and the mouth. Then add the guideline for the pointy sail on Dimetrodon's back.

3. Add the eye and teeth.
Then combine all the basic
shapes into a smooth outline
drawing. Erase any guide-
lines you no longer need.

4. Draw the v
sail. Then ad
within each s
Complete yc
shading and
Dimetrodor

Albertosaurus
(al-BE-tuh-sawr-us)

Means "Alberta Lizard," after the area in Canada where it was found.

Albertosaurus, a relative of Tyrannosaurus, is also known as Gorgosaurus.

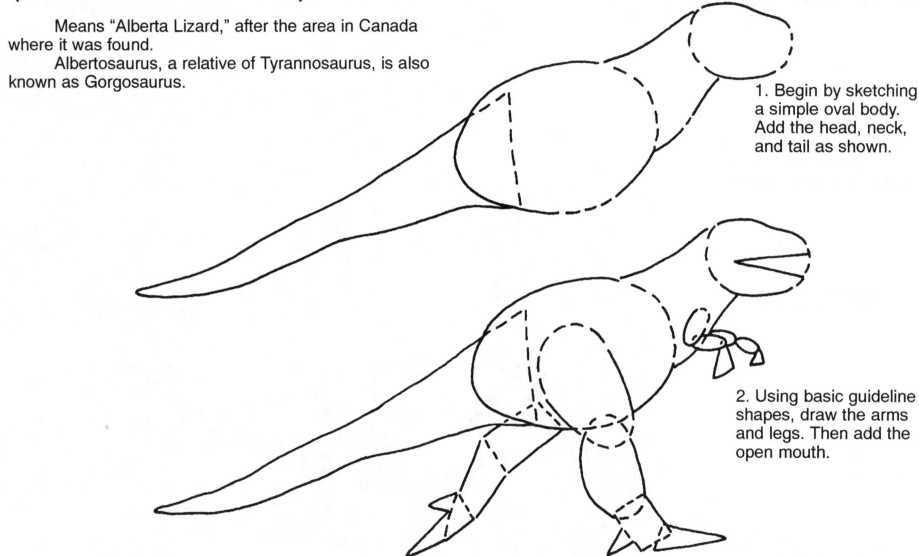

1. Begin by sketching a simple oval body. Add the head, neck, and tail as shown.

2. Using basic guideline shapes, draw the arms and legs. Then add the open mouth.

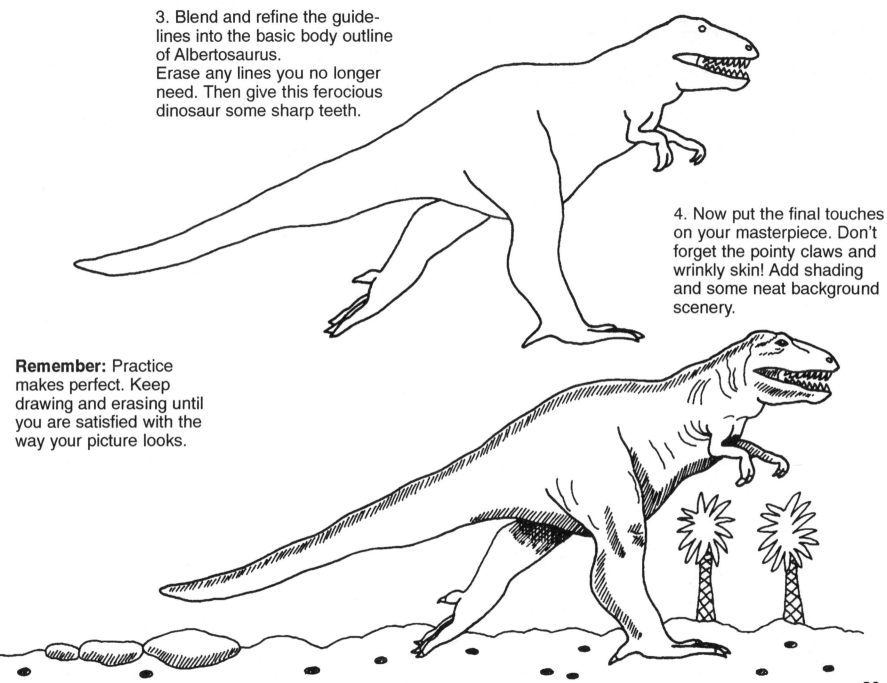

3. Blend and refine the guide-lines into the basic body outline of Albertosaurus.
Erase any lines you no longer need. Then give this ferocious dinosaur some sharp teeth.

4. Now put the final touches on your masterpiece. Don't forget the pointy claws and wrinkly skin! Add shading and some neat background scenery.

Remember: Practice makes perfect. Keep drawing and erasing until you are satisfied with the way your picture looks.

Bagaceratops
(bah-gah-SAIR-uh-tops)

Means "Small Horned Face" because of its small size.
This four-legged plant-eater was only three feet long.

1. Draw a large oval for the body. Then add the basic shapes for the head and horn. Remember to keep these guideline shapes lightly drawn.

2. Add the tail. Next, add the overlapping shapes for the legs and feet.

3. Add the eye and nostril. Combine and blend all the shapes together until you have a complete outline drawing of Bagaceratops.

4. Add lots of details, shading, skin texture, and color for the finishing touches. Then try out some dinosaur footprints!

Apatosaurus
(a-PAT-oh-SAWR-us)

Means "Deceptive Lizard." It is also known as Brontosaurus.

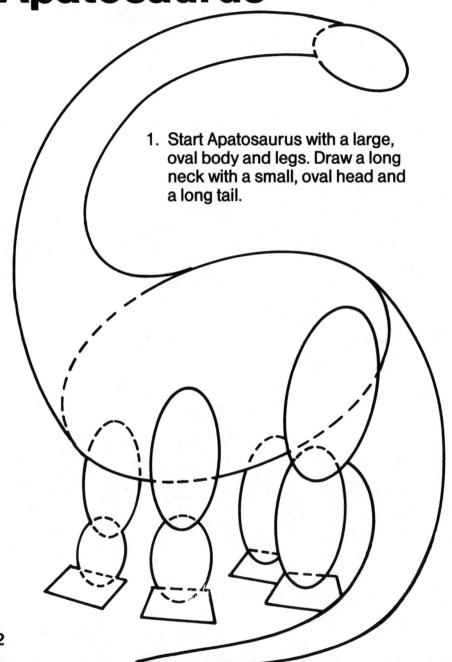

1. Start Apatosaurus with a large, oval body and legs. Draw a long neck with a small, oval head and a long tail.

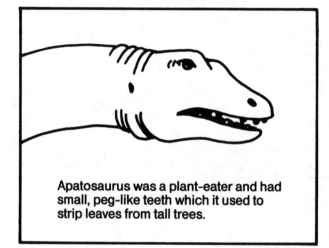

Apatosaurus was a plant-eater and had small, peg-like teeth which it used to strip leaves from tall trees.

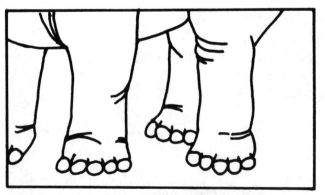

Apatosaurus had thick feet and legs. Its footprints measured nearly 36 inches long and 26 inches wide!

2. Blend all your shapes into one body frame. Erase any unnecessary lines.

3. Add lots of detail, shading, and texture. Put wrinkles on the skin surface, too!

4. Draw some background scenery to complete your drawing.

93

Protoceratops

(pro-toe-SAIR-uh-tops)

Means "First Horned Face" because this was one of the first horned dinosaurs.

1. Start your drawing with 3 basic shapes for the head, body, and tail. Draw guideline shapes lightly.

Protoceratops was in the same family as Triceratops.

2. Next, add 4 legs using ovals and triangles. Did you notice that where the shapes overlap and join, body parts bend and move?

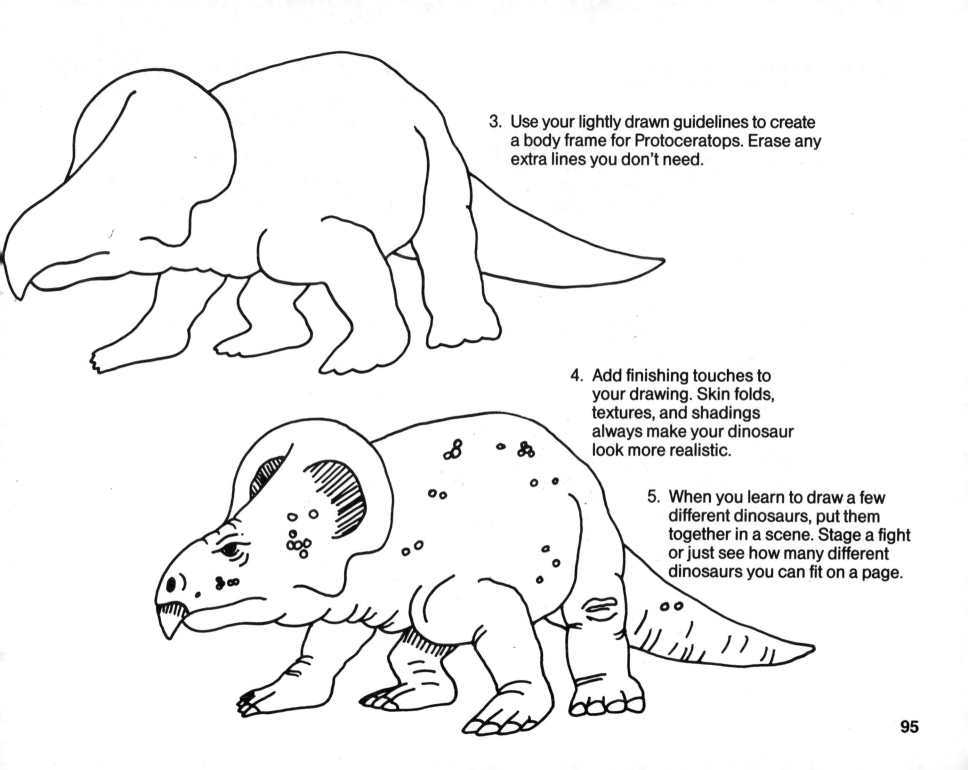

3. Use your lightly drawn guidelines to create a body frame for Protoceratops. Erase any extra lines you don't need.

4. Add finishing touches to your drawing. Skin folds, textures, and shadings always make your dinosaur look more realistic.

5. When you learn to draw a few different dinosaurs, put them together in a scene. Stage a fight or just see how many different dinosaurs you can fit on a page.

Ankylosaurus

(an-kee-luh-SAWR-us)

Means "Stiffened Lizard" and refers to its hard armor-plated body surface.

1. Start your Ankylosaurus with a large oval body. Use ovals as guidelines for its four legs. Use triangles for its feet.

2. Next, add a long triangle for its tail with an oval on the end. Don't forget to add some triangle shapes for "spikes" all over its back.

3. Erase any guidelines you don't need. Add more bumps to its armor-plated back.

4. Now finish your drawing by adding claws to the feet, an eye, bumpy skin, and more!

Pteranodon

(teh-RAN-o-don)

Means "Winged and Toothless" because it could fly and had no teeth.

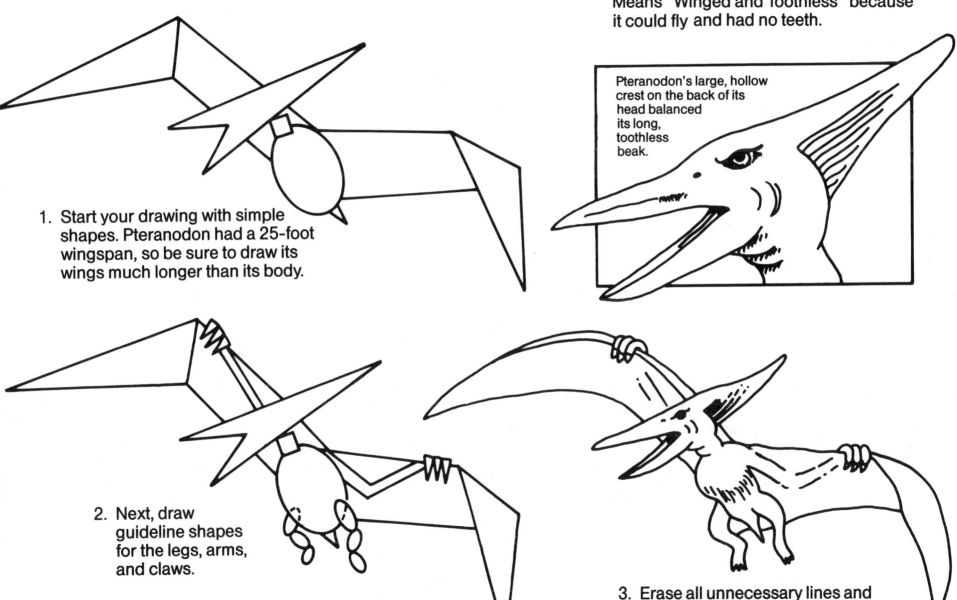

Pteranodon's large, hollow crest on the back of its head balanced its long, toothless beak.

1. Start your drawing with simple shapes. Pteranodon had a 25-foot wingspan, so be sure to draw its wings much longer than its body.

2. Next, draw guideline shapes for the legs, arms, and claws.

3. Erase all unnecessary lines and add lots of details.

Maiasaura

(mah-ee-ah-SAWR-ah)

Means "Good Mother Lizard" because most scientists believe this dinosaur stayed with and cared for her offspring.

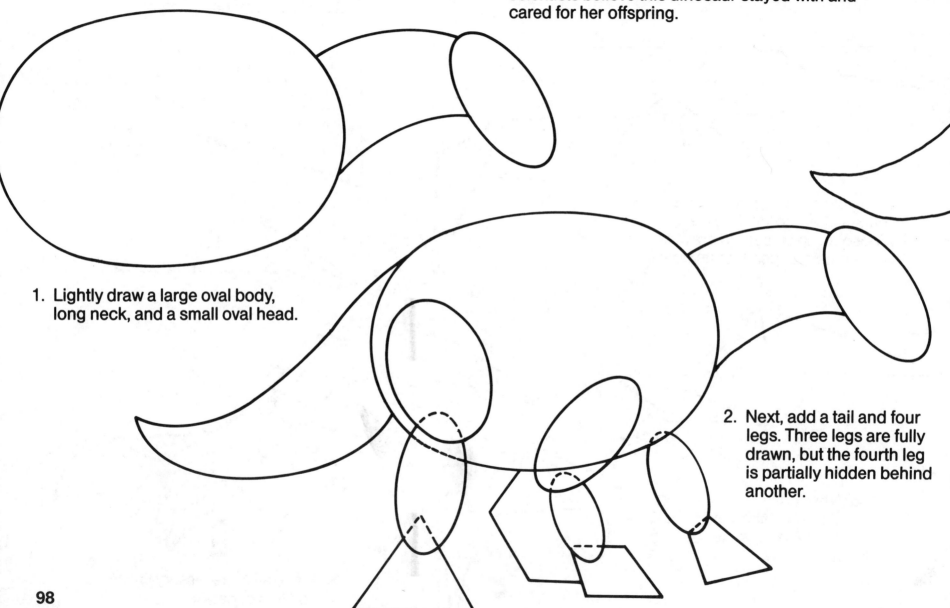

1. Lightly draw a large oval body, long neck, and a small oval head.

2. Next, add a tail and four legs. Three legs are fully drawn, but the fourth leg is partially hidden behind another.

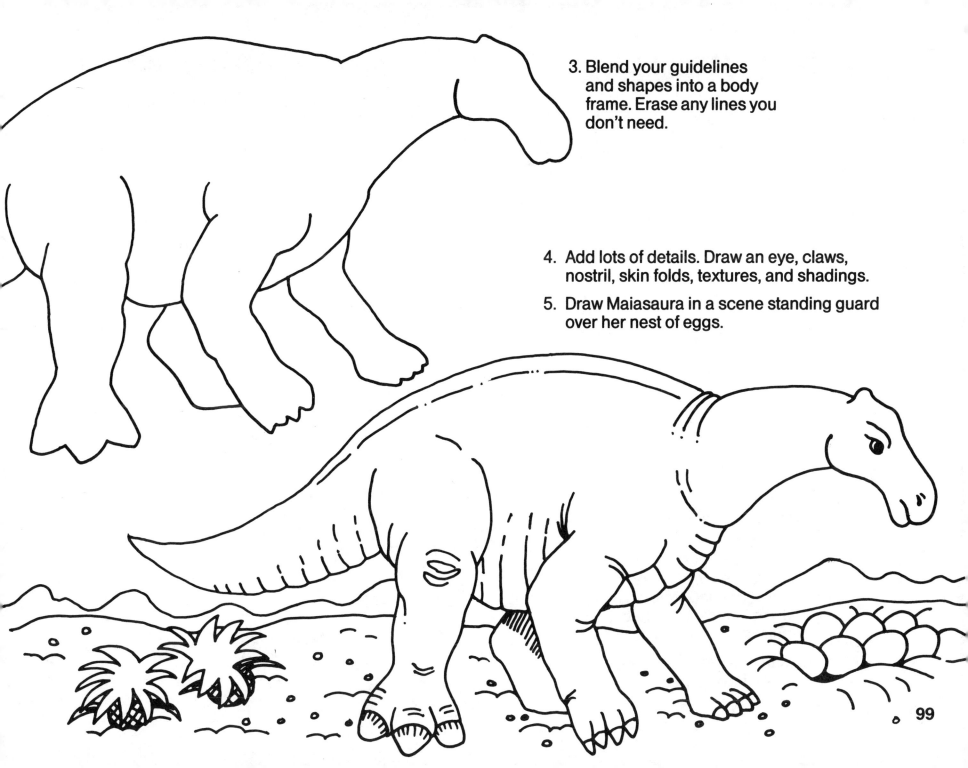

3. Blend your guidelines and shapes into a body frame. Erase any lines you don't need.

4. Add lots of details. Draw an eye, claws, nostril, skin folds, textures, and shadings.

5. Draw Maiasaura in a scene standing guard over her nest of eggs.

99

Corythosaurus

(KO-RITH-uh-sawr-us)

Means "Helmet Lizard" and refers to the shape of the bony crest on its head.

1. Start your dinosaur drawing with basic shapes (ovals and circles) for the head, neck, and body. These are only guidelines, so draw them in lightly.

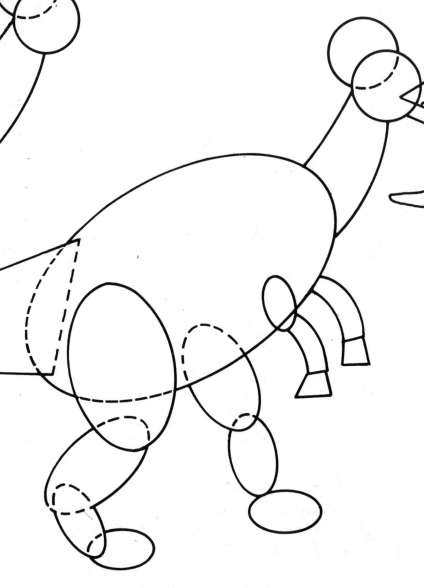

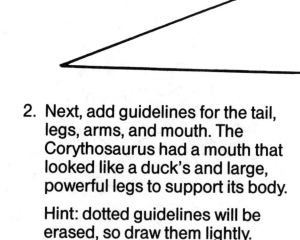

2. Next, add guidelines for the tail, legs, arms, and mouth. The Corythosaurus had a mouth that looked like a duck's and large, powerful legs to support its body.

   Hint: dotted guidelines will be erased, so draw them lightly.

100

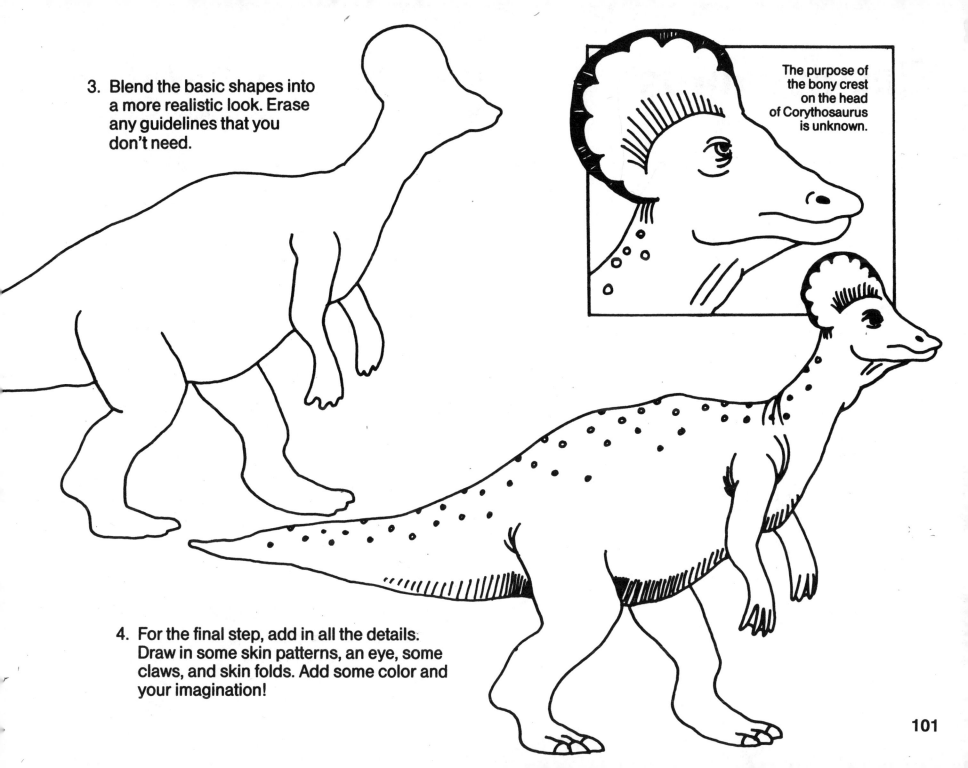

3. Blend the basic shapes into a more realistic look. Erase any guidelines that you don't need.

The purpose of the bony crest on the head of Corythosaurus is unknown.

4. For the final step, add in all the details. Draw in some skin patterns, an eye, some claws, and skin folds. Add some color and your imagination!

Elasmosaurus

(ee-LAZ-muh-SAWR-us)

Means "Thin-plated Lizard" and refers to a marine reptile, not a dinosaur.

1. Start your drawing with a large oval for the body and 4 small ovals for its flippers.

2. Next, add a long tail and a very, very long neck, with a small oval-shaped head. Elasmosaurus measured more than 40 feet in length!

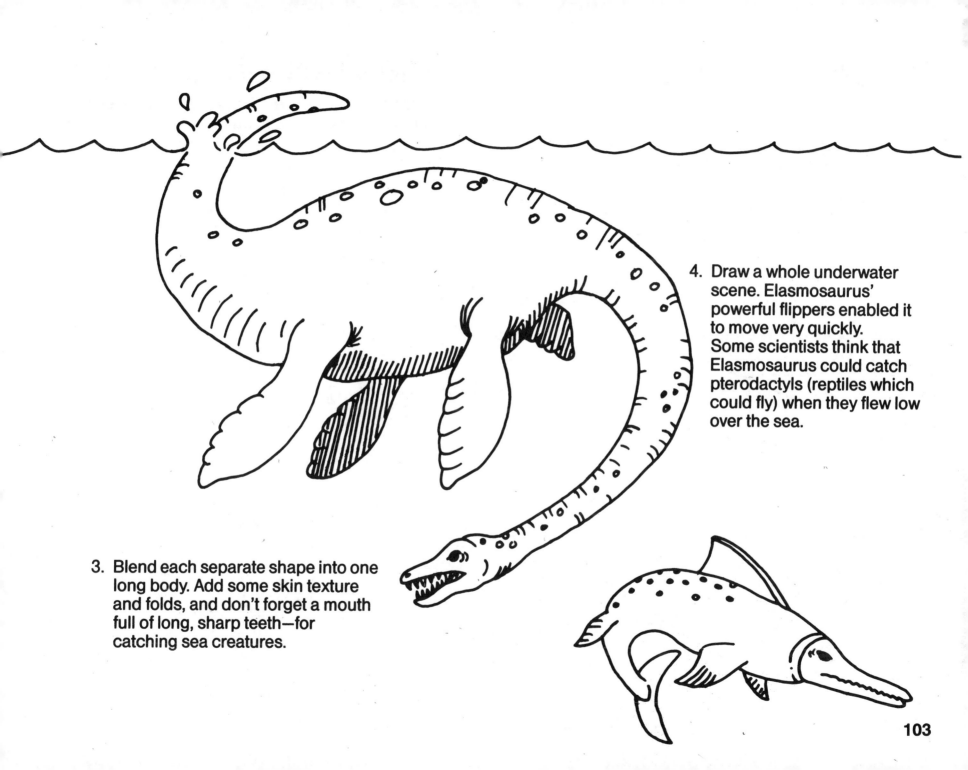

4. Draw a whole underwater scene. Elasmosaurus' powerful flippers enabled it to move very quickly. Some scientists think that Elasmosaurus could catch pterodactyls (reptiles which could fly) when they flew low over the sea.

3. Blend each separate shape into one long body. Add some skin texture and folds, and don't forget a mouth full of long, sharp teeth—for catching sea creatures.

Tyrannosaurus

(tie-RAN-uh-sawr-us)

Means "Tyrant Lizard" and refers to the largest known meat-eating dinosaur.

1. Use rectangles, squares, ovals, circles, and triangles for the head, body, and tail. Remember, since these are only guidelines, draw them lightly.

2. Using basic shapes as your guide, add small forearms and large hind legs.

   Hint: all dotted guidelines will be erased, so draw them extra lightly.

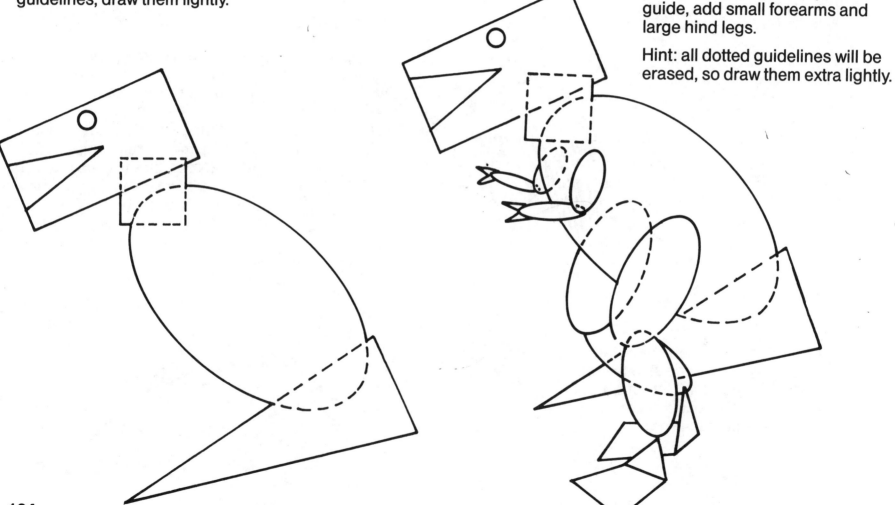

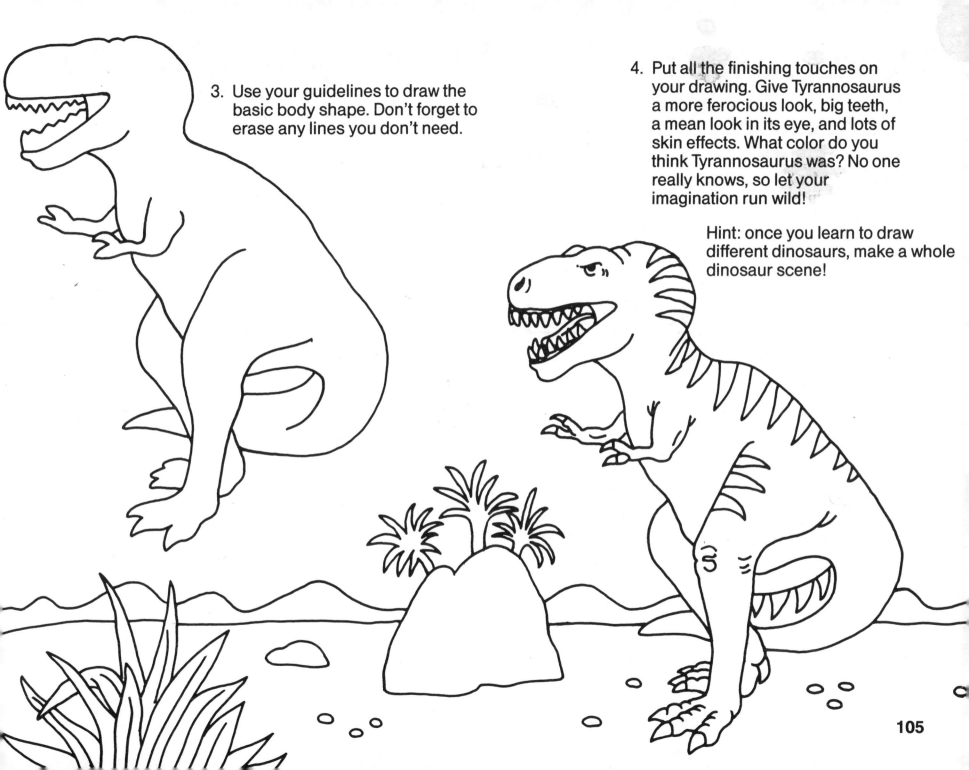

3. Use your guidelines to draw the basic body shape. Don't forget to erase any lines you don't need.

4. Put all the finishing touches on your drawing. Give Tyrannosaurus a more ferocious look, big teeth, a mean look in its eye, and lots of skin effects. What color do you think Tyrannosaurus was? No one really knows, so let your imagination run wild!

Hint: once you learn to draw different dinosaurs, make a whole dinosaur scene!

105

Dromaeosaurus

(drom-ee-uh-SAWR-us)

Means "Swift Lizard" because this fast, fierce dinosaur ran upright on powerful hind legs.

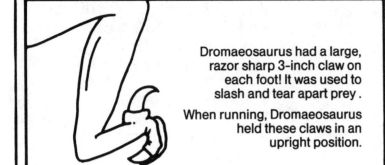

Dromaeosaurus had a large, razor sharp 3-inch claw on each foot! It was used to slash and tear apart prey .

When running, Dromaeosaurus held these claws in an upright position.

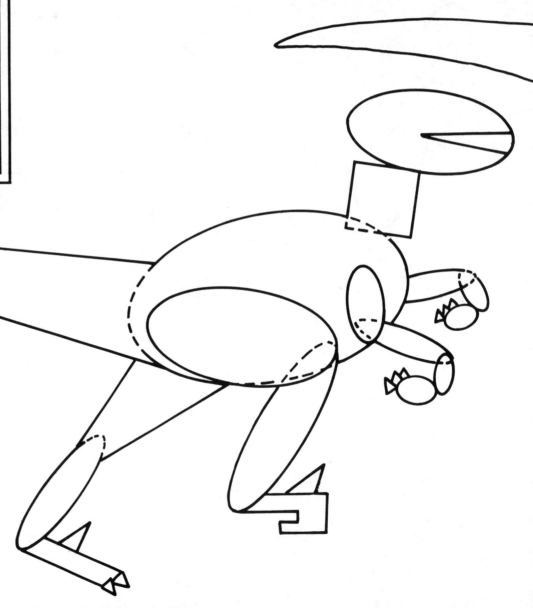

1. Try to draw this dinosaur in just three steps. Use simple shapes for the body of your Dromaeosaurus. Lightly sketch the tail, neck, head, arms, and legs. Put some triangles in as guidelines for claws.

2. Blend your basic shapes into a body shape. Erase guidelines you don't need.

3. Finish your dinosaur by adding important details. Draw skin folds where Dromaeosaurus' arms and legs bend. Add an eye, a nostril, teeth, and claws. Really use your imagination to draw some skin markings, textures, and colors.

Stegosaurus

(steg-uh-SAWR-us)

Means "Plated Lizard" and refers to the rows of plates on its back.

1. Start drawing your Stegosaurus with these basic shapes: ovals and a triangle.

Always draw your guidelines lightly—they'll be easier to erase.

2. Draw some triangles on its tail and diamond-shaped plates on its back. Use ovals for the legs.

Hint: a diamond shape is made by putting 2 triangles together like this:

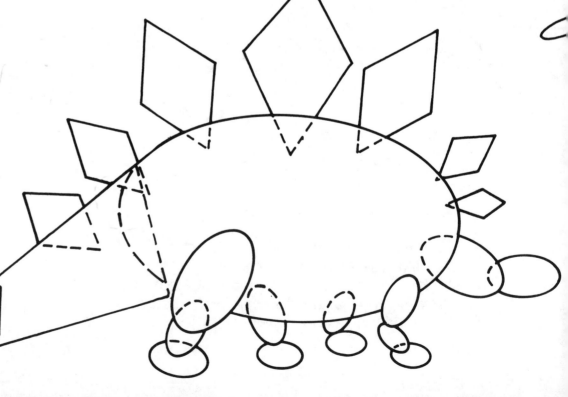

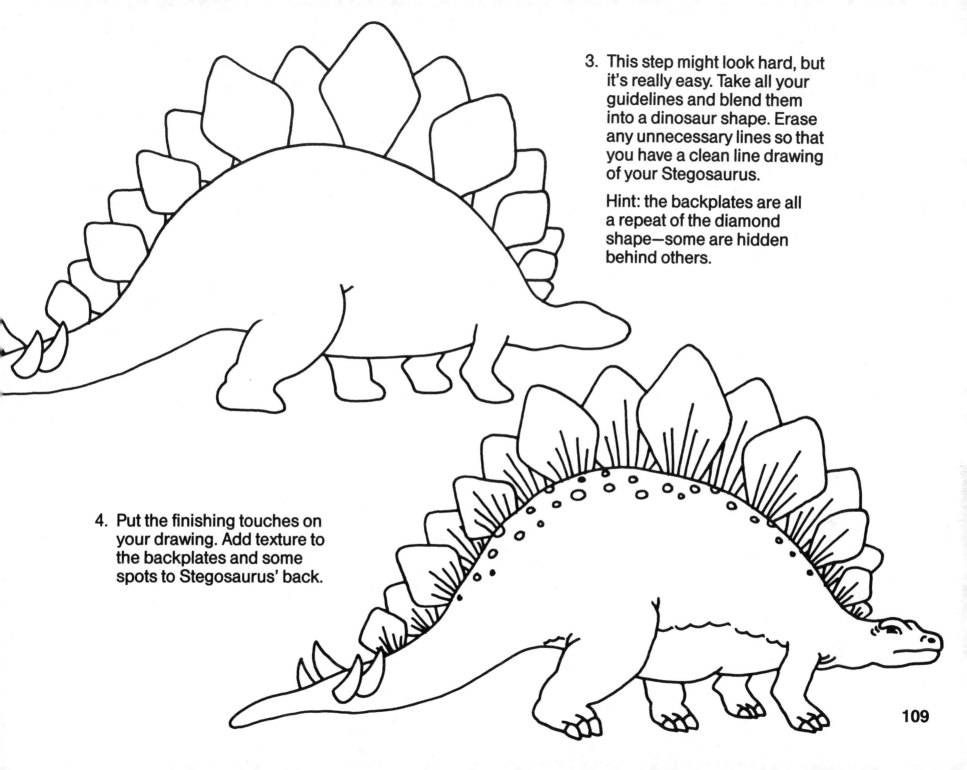

3. This step might look hard, but it's really easy. Take all your guidelines and blend them into a dinosaur shape. Erase any unnecessary lines so that you have a clean line drawing of your Stegosaurus.

Hint: the backplates are all a repeat of the diamond shape—some are hidden behind others.

4. Put the finishing touches on your drawing. Add texture to the backplates and some spots to Stegosaurus' back.

109

Saltopus

(SALT-o-pus)

Means "Leaping Foot" and refers to the way that Saltopus ran upright on its hind legs.

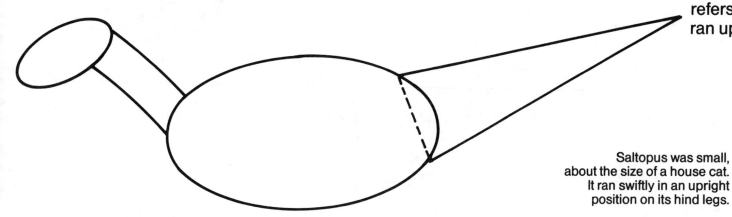

Saltopus was small, about the size of a house cat. It ran swiftly in an upright position on its hind legs.

1. Start your drawing with an oval body, long triangle-shaped tail, long neck, and oval head.

2. Next, add small arms, long hind legs, and feet.

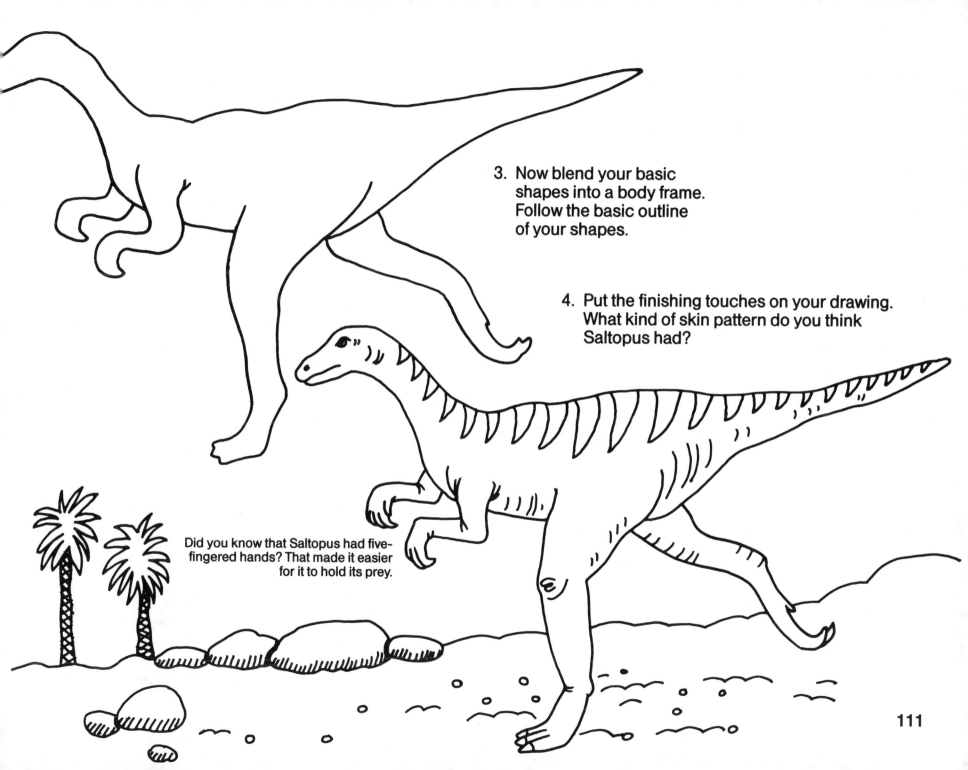

3. Now blend your basic
   shapes into a body frame.
   Follow the basic outline
   of your shapes.

4. Put the finishing touches on your drawing.
   What kind of skin pattern do you think
   Saltopus had?

Did you know that Saltopus had five-
fingered hands? That made it easier
for it to hold its prey.

Parasaurolophus

(par-uh-SAWR-OL-uh-fus)

Means "Similiar-Crested Lizard."

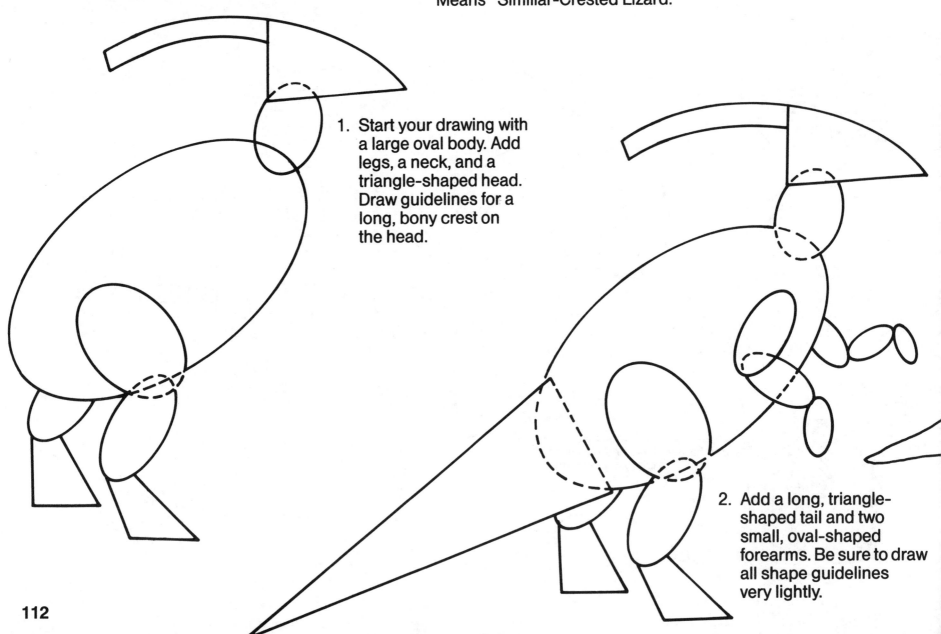

1. Start your drawing with a large oval body. Add legs, a neck, and a triangle-shaped head. Draw guidelines for a long, bony crest on the head.

2. Add a long, triangle-shaped tail and two small, oval-shaped forearms. Be sure to draw all shape guidelines very lightly.

3. Now blend all your guideline shapes into a body frame.

The purpose of the long, bony crest on the head of the Parasaurolophus is not known. Some scientists think the crest helped the animal's sense of smell. Others think the crest may have been used to make loud sounds.

4. Add claws, an eye, nostril, and lots of skin folds, shading, and texture.

113

Pachycephalosaurus
(pack-ee-SEF-al-owe-saw-rus)

Means "Reptile with a Thick Head" because the bone on top of its head was 10 inches thick!

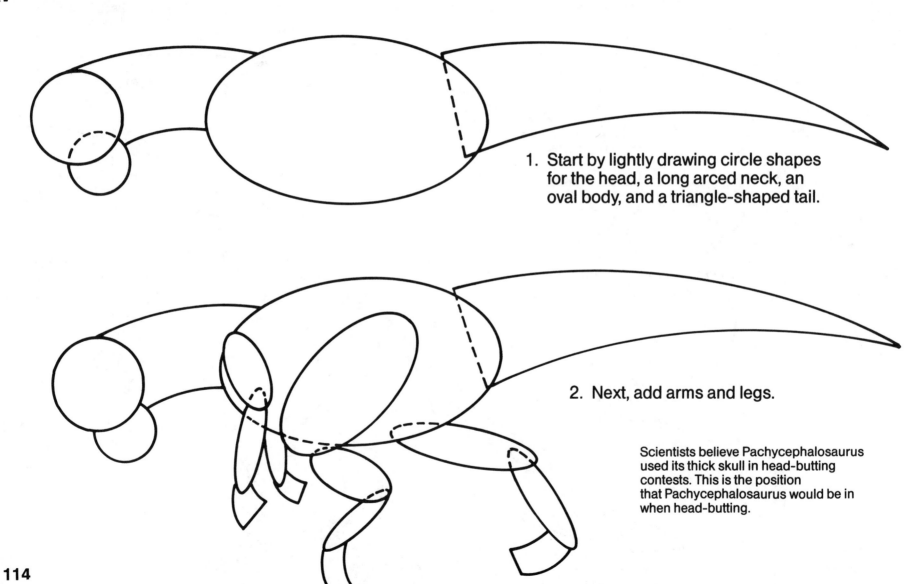

1. Start by lightly drawing circle shapes for the head, a long arced neck, an oval body, and a triangle-shaped tail.

2. Next, add arms and legs.

Scientists believe Pachycephalosaurus used its thick skull in head-butting contests. This is the position that Pachycephalosaurus would be in when head-butting.

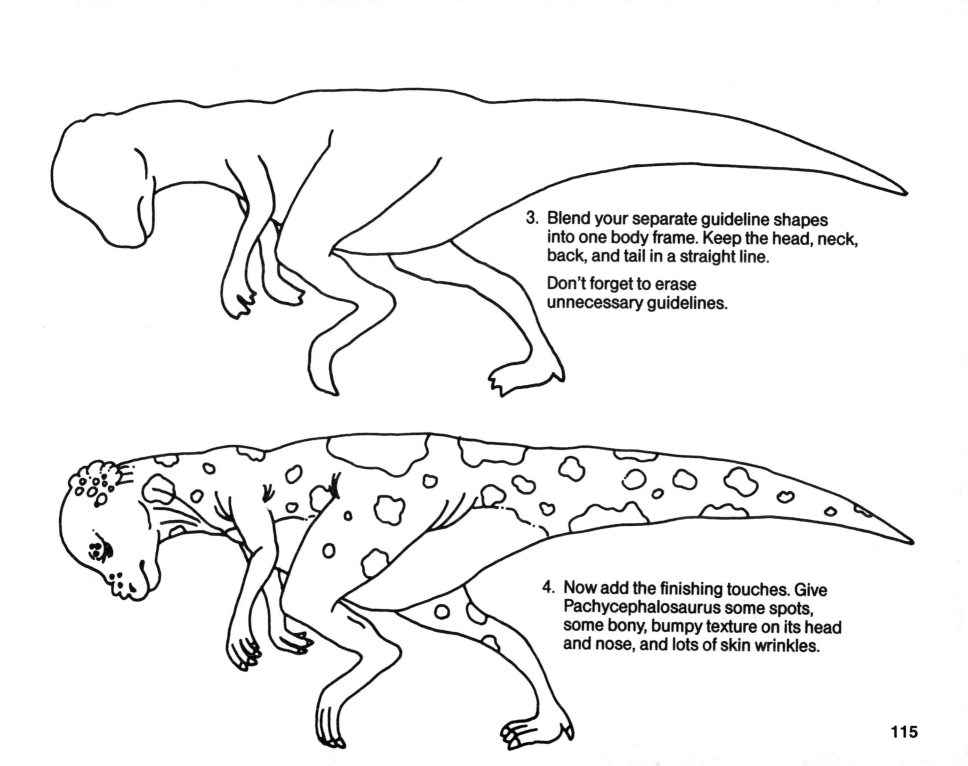

3. Blend your separate guideline shapes into one body frame. Keep the head, neck, back, and tail in a straight line.

Don't forget to erase unnecessary guidelines.

4. Now add the finishing touches. Give Pachycephalosaurus some spots, some bony, bumpy texture on its head and nose, and lots of skin wrinkles.

Triceratops

Means "Three-horned Face." It was one of the last dinosaurs to become extinct.

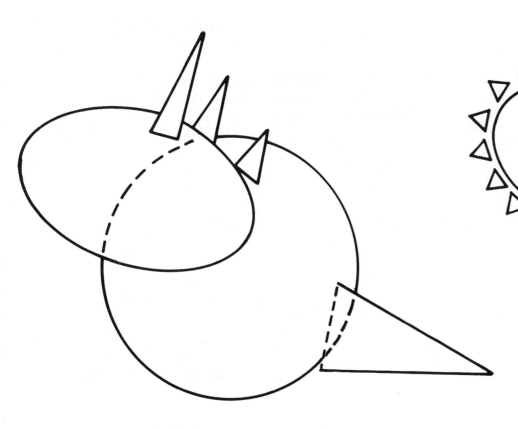

1. Start drawing Triceratops using an oval, triangles, and a circle. It's easy to draw anything when you break it down to simple shapes!

2. Add 4 legs using oval and triangle shapes. See how the legs bend where the shapes meet each other? Add some triangles around the back of the head, too.

116

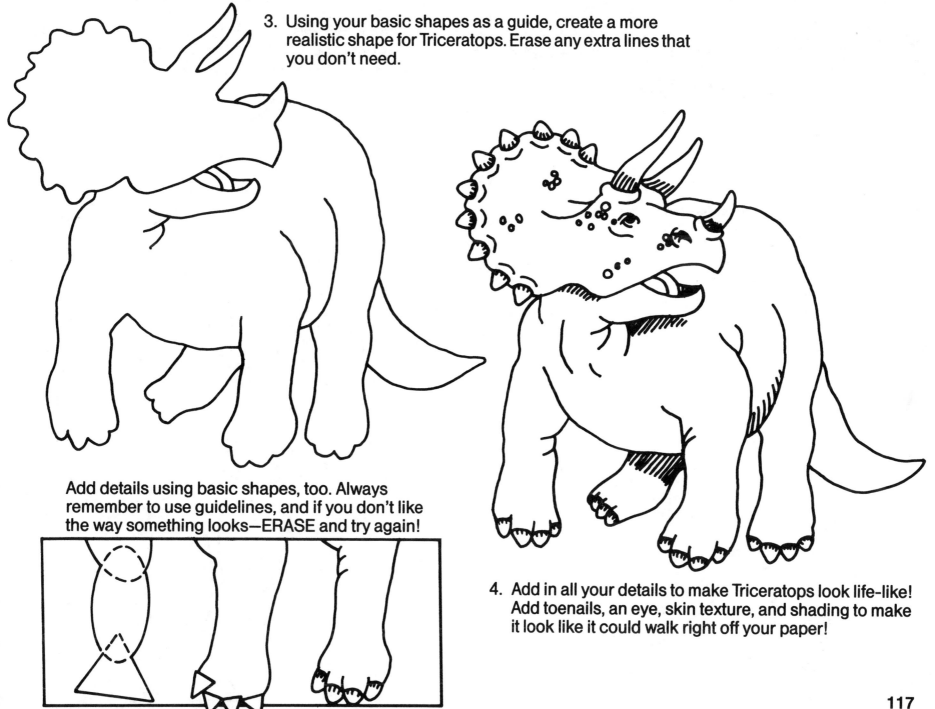

3. Using your basic shapes as a guide, create a more realistic shape for Triceratops. Erase any extra lines that you don't need.

Add details using basic shapes, too. Always remember to use guidelines, and if you don't like the way something looks—ERASE and try again!

4. Add in all your details to make Triceratops look life-like! Add toenails, an eye, skin texture, and shading to make it look like it could walk right off your paper!

117

Spinosaurus
(SPY-no-saw-rus)

Means "Spiny Lizard" and refers to the very long spines on this dinosaur's back.

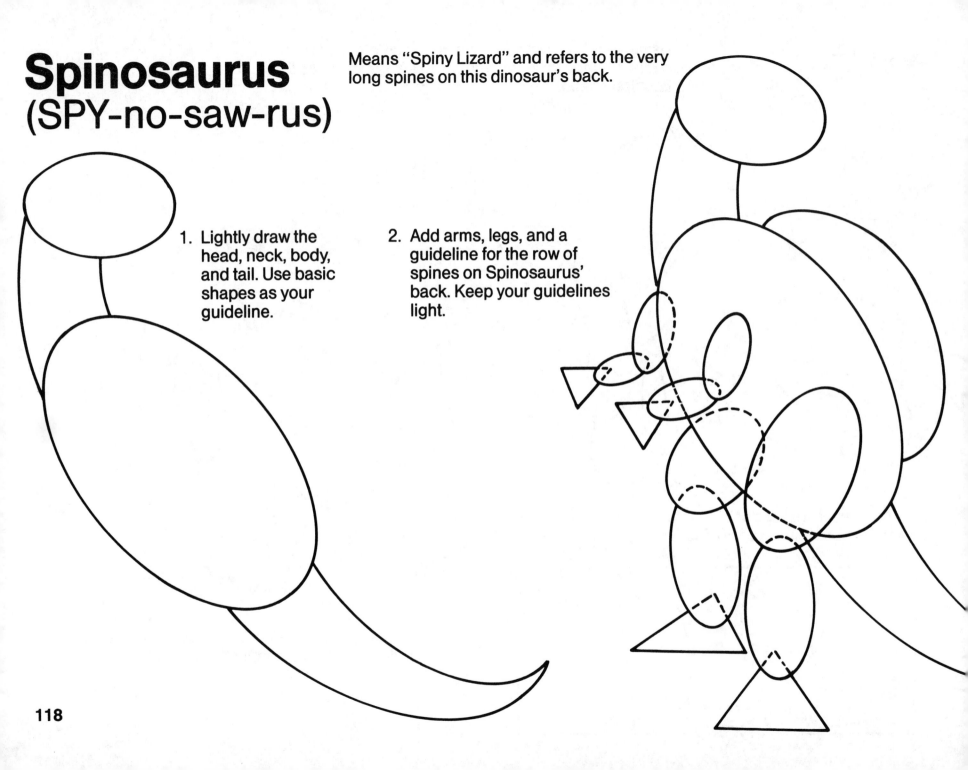

1. Lightly draw the head, neck, body, and tail. Use basic shapes as your guideline.

2. Add arms, legs, and a guideline for the row of spines on Spinosaurus' back. Keep your guidelines light.

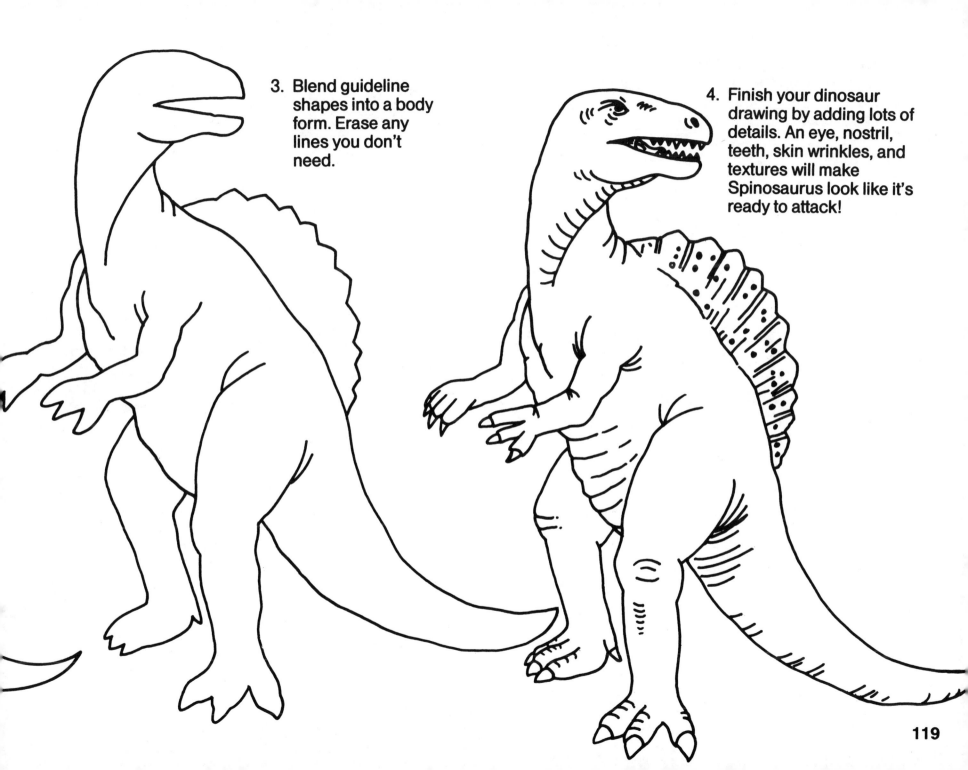

3. Blend guideline shapes into a body form. Erase any lines you don't need.

4. Finish your dinosaur drawing by adding lots of details. An eye, nostril, teeth, skin wrinkles, and textures will make Spinosaurus look like it's ready to attack!

Use your imagination to fill these
scenes with some of the
dinosaurs you've learned to
draw. Draw some
plant-eating
dinosaurs
as well as
some meat-
eaters.

INDEX

CERATOSAURUS P.26

IGUANODON P.28

AVIMIMUS P.30

ICHTHYOSAURUS P.32

COELOPHYSIS P.33

OVIRAPTOR P.34

TYLOSAURUS P.36

LAMBEOSAURUS P.38

ALLOSAURUS P.40

CHASMOSAURUS P.42

STENONYCHOSAURUS P.44   **ARCHAEOPTERYX P.46**   **NODOSAURUS P.48**   **OURANOSAURUS P.50**   **BRACHIOSAURUS P.52**

PSITTACOSAURUS P.54   **DINICHTHYS P.56**   **FABROSAURUS P.58**   **HETERODONTOSAURUS P.60**   **TARBOSAURUS P.62**

CHIALINGOSAURUS P.64　　**MEGALOSAURUS P.66**　　**ANATOSAURUS P.68**　　**ARCHELON P.70**　　**LEPTOCERATOPS P.72**

DILOPHOSAURUS P.74　**RHAMPHORHYNCHUS P.76**　**HYLAEOSAURUS P.78**　**DEINONYCHUS P.80**　**METRIORHYNCHUS P.82**

DIMETRODON P.84   ANTARCTOSAURUS P.86   ALBERTOSAURUS P.88   BAGACERATOPS P.90   APATOSAURUS P.92

PROTOCERATOPS P.94   ANKYLOSAURUS P.96   PTERANODON P.97   MAIASAURA P.98   CORYTHOSAURUS P.100

ELASMOSAURUS P.102   TYRANNOSAURUS P.104   DROMAEOSAURUS P.106   STEGOSAURUS P.108   SALTOPUS P.110

PARASAUROLOPHUS P.112   PACHYCEPHALOSAURUS P.114   TRICERATOPS P.116   SPINOSAURUS P.118   SCENERY P.120